L

On

Microorganisms
& Biotechnology

ADVANCED
BIOLOGY
READERS

Peter
Chenn

**JOHN
MURRAY**

First published in 1997
by John Murray (Publishers) Ltd
50 Albemarle Street
London W1X 4BD

Layouts by Black Dog Design.
Illustrations by Art Construction and Jeff Edwards.
Cover design by John Townson/Creation.

Typeset in 11.5/13pt Goudy by Wearset, Boldon, Tyne and Wear.
Printed and bound in Great Britain by Alden Press, Osney Mead, Oxford.

A catalogue record for this book is available from the British Library.

ISBN 0 7195 7509 5

Contents

Introduction

Biotechnology is a branch of biology that is advancing at what appears at times to be a bewilderingly fast pace. We read about how scientists have developed the ultimate cash crop – plants that produce plastic polymers that can be used to make biodegradable bin liners and bottles; how researchers in Australia have succeeded in genetically modifying a vine to produce superior grapes with enhanced flavours, improved colour development and resistance to disease. The latest controversy to grab media attention has been the published photographs of sheep brought into this world not by the usual process of sexual reproduction but by cloning. It has raised moral debate and brought suspicion against biotechnologists, with visions of a future world inhabited by cloned humans, programmed from the laboratory by white-coated scientists.

This book has a rather humble beginning. It began when recent syllabus changes sent the author, as a teacher of Advanced level biology, to look for information not available in the standard A level biology textbooks but which was needed in order to teach several newly introduced topics. The information was, of course, available in recent scientific journals but in a form that was too detailed and complicated for the ordinary A level biology student. It had to be gleaned out of the journals and then written in a form that the author's A level students could easily understand. From the 'notes' that were supplied to his students, the author became involved, with the encouragement of his publishers John Murray, in writing the *Advanced Biology Readers* series of which *Microorganisms & Biotechnology* is the first.

To the A level student taking the Biotechnology (and Microorganisms) unit or module as one of his/her A level biology options, this book intends to be enjoyable to read, as well as being informative, interesting and up-to-date. The style is aimed at students of mixed ability, and the illustrations are designed for simplicity and relevance. The information builds on prior knowledge of cells, proteins, enzymes, DNA structure, protein synthesis and basic genetics, including knowledge of gene and chromosomal mutation.

Acknowledgements

I owe my greatest indebtedness to the numerous scientists and researchers who have contributed to the *New Scientist, Scientific American* and the *Biological Review*; without their work this book would not have been possible. I am also indebted to Chris Clegg, co-author of *Advanced Biology: Principles and Applications*, for reading the manuscript and for his useful suggestions during the preparation of this book. I would like to express my thanks to the team at John Murray, especially Katie Mackenzie Stuart (Science Publisher) for her guidance and encouragement and Nikki Taylor for her skilful editing, and, not least, my family. Finally, thanks to my A level students for being my guinea pigs.

Examination questions

Exam questions have been reproduced with kind permission from the following examination boards:
Welsh Joint Education Committee (WJEC)
Oxford and Cambridge Schools Examination Board (O & C)
University of Oxford Delegacy of Local Examinations (UODLE)
London Examinations, A division of EdExcel Foundation (ULEAC)
Northern Examinations and Assessment board (NEAB)
University of Cambridge Local Examinations Syndicate (UCLES)
Associated Examining Board (AEB)

Source acknowledgements

The following are sources from which artwork has been redrawn:
Figure 1.10, page 8 Cell wall structure of Gram-negative bacteria (lower diagram) – Ernst Theodor Rietschel and Helmut Brade, 'Bacterial Endotoxins', *Scientific American* (August 1992) page 28
Figure 1.18, page 15 Keith Vickeman and Francis E.G. Cox, *Paramecium – The Protozoa* (John Murray, 1967) page 46
Figure 3.2, page 38 Drawings of Antony van Leeuwenhoek's simple microscope – C. Dobell, *Antony Leeuwenhoek and his "Little Animals"* (Dover Publications Inc., New York)
Figure 3.9, page 44 A summary of Paul Berg's experiment – Stanley N. Cohen, 'The manipulation of genes', *Scientific American* (July 1975) page 27
Figure 4.1, page 46 A bioreactor – Elmer L. Gaden, Jr, 'Production methods in Industrial Microbiology', *Scientific American* (September 1981) page 139
Figure 4.4, page 53 Commercial production of beer – Harry Epton, 'Brewing', *Biological Sciences Review* (January 1993) page 11
Figure 4.8, page 59 The production of 'Pruteen' (single-cell protein) – David Dawson, 'Bacterial Biomass as food!' *Biologial Sciences Review* (May 1991) page 35
Figure 4.9, page 61 An airlift fermenter for the continuous culture of *Fusarium graminearum* – Tony Trinci, 'Food From Fungus', *Biological Sciences Review* (November 1989) page 14
Figure 5.5, page 73 Procedure for identifying the insulin-secreting clones –Walter Gilbert and Lydia Villa Komaroff, 'Useful Proteins from Recombinant Bacteria', *Scientific American* (April 1980) page 80
Figure 5.7, page 76 Blocking the production of polygalacturonase – Susan Katz Miller, 'Genetic first upsets food lobby', *New Scientist* (28 May 1994)
Figure 5.8, page 77 Using the bacterium *Agrobacterium tumefaciens* to genetically engineer plants – Mary Dell Chilton, 'A Vector for Introducing New Genes into Plants', *Scientific American* (June 1983) page 43
Figure 6.5, page 86 Sequence of events leading to the establishment of a symbiotic relationship between *Rhizobium* and a leguminous plant – Winston Brill, 'Agricultural microbiology', *Scientific American* (September 1981) page 149
Figure 6.9, page 92 A biogas plant (Indian design) – Robert jon Lichtman, *Biogas Systems in India*, COSTED Central Leath Research Institute, Madras, India
Figure 7.1, page 107 Methods of enzyme immobilisation – *Encyclopedia of Polymer Science and Engineering*, 2nd ed. (Volume 6) page 183, figure 25
Figure 7.2, page 109 A flow diagram for the immobilisation of glucose isomerase – *Encyclopedia of Polymer Science and Engineering*, 2nd ed. (Volume 6) page 164, figure 18
Figure 7.3, page 110 The continuous production of lactose-free milk – *Encyclopedia of Polymer Science and Engineering* (Volume 6) page 169, figure 21

Figure 8.2, page 119 Procedure for monoclonal antibody production – Cesar Milstein, 'Monoclonal Antibodies', *Scientific American* (October 1980) page 61

Figure 8.3, page 120 Using monoclonal antibodies to purify interferon – Sidney Pestka, 'The Purification and Manufacture of Human Interferon', *Scientific American* (August 1983) page 33

Figure 8.5, page 122 A glucose biosensor – Pankaj Vadgama, 'Biosensors – Artificial Sniffer dogs!', *Biological Sciences Review* (May 1989) page 39

Figure 8.6, page 124 DNA fingerprinting – Peter Martin, 'Genetic profiling in forensic science', *Biological Sciences Review* (May 1995) page 39

Figure 9.4, page 137 HIV's cell infection cycle – Martin A. Nowak and Andrew J. McMichael, 'How HIV defeats the Immune System', *Scientific American* (August 1995) page 44

Photo credits

Thanks are due to the following for permission to reproduce copyright photographs:

Cover: Science Photo Library
Figure 1.3, page 3 Nigel Cattlin/Holt Studios International
Figure 1.4, page 3 Eye of Science/Science Photo Library
Figure 1.5, page 4 Eye of Science/Science Photo Library
Figure 1.7, page 5 Institut Pasteur/CNRI/Science Photo Library
Figure 1.14, page 12 CNRI/Science Photo Library
Figure 1.16, page 13 Dr L. Caro/Science Photo Library
Figure 1.21, page 17 J. Forsdyke/Gene Cox/Science Photo Library
Figure 1.25a, page 19 left, Biophoto Associates/Science Photo Library
Figure 1.25b, page 19 right, Dr Judy Brangeon, Oxford and Cambridge Schools Examination Board
Figure 3.1, page 37 Mary Evans Picture Library
Figure 3.3, page 38 Custom Medical Stock Photo/Science Photo Library
Figure 3.4, page 39 Custom Medical Stock Photo/Science Photo Library
Figure 3.6, page 42 St Mary's Hospital Medical School/Science Photo Library
Figure 3.7, page 42 St Mary's Hospital Medical School/Science Photo Library
Figure 3.8, page 43 Camera Press Ltd
Figure 3.10, page 46 Robert H. Devlin, Fisheries And Oceans Canada
Figure 4.5, page 54 Norman Hollands/New Crane Publishing Ltd
Figure 4.13, page 64 C. Higgins, Best & Jones, *Biotechnology: principles and applications* (Figure 3.5, page 101) Blackwell Science Ltd
Figure 5.2, page 70 Prof Stanley Cohen/Science Photo Library
Figure 5.6, page 74 Holt Studios International
Figure 6.1a, page 84 left, Nigel Cattlin/Holt Studios International
Figure 6.1b, page 84 right, Nigel Cattlin/Holt Studios International
Figure 6.2, page 84 Monsanto Europe, S.A., Belgium
Figure 6.3, page 85 Dr Jeremy Burgess/Science Photo Library
Figure 6.4a, page 86 left, Dr Jeremy Burgess/Science Photo Library
Figure 6.4b, page 86 right, Dr Jeremy Burgess/Science Photo Library
Figure 6.7, page 90 Stephanie Maze, Woodfin Camp And Associates
Figure 6.8, page 90 Professor David Hall, King's College London
Figure 6.11, page 99 Simon Fraser/Science Photo Library
Figure 6.12, page 100 Monsanto Europe S.A., Belgium
Figure 8.8, page 127 Simon Fraser/RVI, Newcastle-Upon-Tyne/Science Photo Library
Figure 9.1, page 134 Mary Evans Picture Library
Figure 9.7, page 140 Dr Kari Lounatmaa/Science Photo Library
Figure 9.9, page 143 Will & Demi McIntyre/Science Photo Library
Figure 9.11, page 148 Mary Evans Picture Library
Figure 9.12, page 148 Mary Evans Picture Library
Figure 9.13, page 151 Wellcome Institute Library, London

Range of microorganisms

Viruses

Viruses are tiny infectious agents that carry the genetic message 'reproduce me' from one cell to another and usually manifest their presence by causing disease. Many of the most important human diseases, including hepatitis, AIDS, influenza, common cold, mumps, measles, chickenpox, rabies and rubella (German measles), are caused by viruses.

Viruses range in size from 0.02 to 0.4 micrometres (μm). They cannot feed, respire, excrete, grow, move or respond to stimuli. They are chemicals that 'live' as cell parasites. After gaining entry into a host cell, the virus can direct the cell's biosynthetic machinery to make copies of itself.

Structure

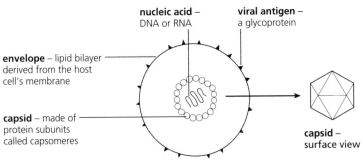

nucleic acid – DNA or RNA

viral antigen – a glycoprotein

envelope – lipid bilayer derived from the host cell's membrane

capsid – made of protein subunits called capsomeres

capsid – surface view

Figure 1.1 Structure of a virus

Each virus particle consists of one or more strands of **nucleic acid** enclosed within a **protein coat** or **capsid**. The capsid is composed of protein subunits known as **capsomeres**. Some viruses also have a membranous lipid **envelope** surrounding the capsid and this is derived from the host cell's membrane.

Classification

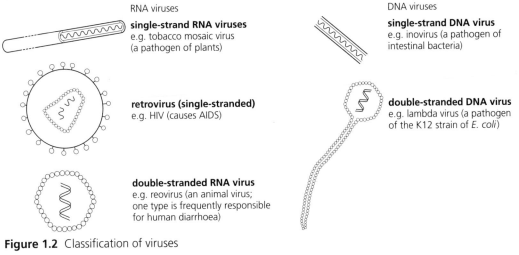

RNA viruses

single-strand RNA viruses
e.g. tobacco mosaic virus (a pathogen of plants)

retrovirus (single-stranded)
e.g. HIV (causes AIDS)

double-stranded RNA virus
e.g. reovirus (an animal virus; one type is frequently responsible for human diarrhoea)

DNA viruses

single-strand DNA virus
e.g. inovirus (a pathogen of intestinal bacteria)

double-stranded DNA virus
e.g. lambda virus (a pathogen of the K12 strain of *E. coli*)

Figure 1.2 Classification of viruses

Viruses are classified on the basis of their nucleic acid into two main groups – **DNA viruses** and **RNA viruses**. Both groups can be subdivided further into **single-** or **double-stranded** viruses depending on whether their nucleic acid exists as single- or double-stranded molecules. The shape of the capsid can also be used as a basis for classification.

Virus–host cell interaction

Before a virus can do any harm, it must gain entry into a host cell. Infection begins when proteins on the outer surface of the virus bind on to specific receptors on the host cell's surface. The attraction between the viral proteins (known as antigens) and the host receptor sites is highly specific, even closely related viruses will bind on to different receptors. The binding triggers a reaction that results in the entry of the viral genetic material into the host cell.

The infection that follows can be subdivided into two main types – **lytic interactions** and **transforming interactions**.

Lytic interaction

Lytic interactions are characteristic of most viral infections, including the common cold and polio. The virus replicates within the host cell by causing it to make copies of the viral genetic material and viral proteins. Shortly after infection, the host cell **lyses** (ruptures) releasing a multitude of new virus particles. When a virus infects a multicellular organism, this process of viral replication followed by cell lysis may occur several times until the body's defences gain the upper hand or until the host organism dies.

Transforming interaction

In transforming interaction, the virus 'lives' within the host cell without destroying it. Viral replication is suppressed and the viral genetic material becomes what is known as a **provirus** by incorporating itself into the DNA of one of the host cell's chromosomes. In this way, it can be passively replicated and passed on at each cell division as a part of the host cell's DNA. The host cells are, in this way, transformed by the virus, and the infection can continue for months or years without any overt signs of disease. Herpes simplex and hepatitis B are examples of viruses that lie dormant and undetected for long periods before flaring up as painful or life-threatening diseases. Transformed animal and plant cells can in some cases develop into tumours.

Tobacco mosaic virus

The tobacco mosaic virus (TMV) is a single-stranded RNA virus. It has a capsid of protein subunits arranged in a helix to form a rod-shaped tube. Its genetic material consists of a corkscrew-shaped RNA molecule running through the hollow centre of the capsid.

TMV attacks a wide range of plant species. It causes distortion, blistering and mottling (light and dark-green patches) of leaves. It can be transmitted from plant to plant on the mouthparts of sap-sucking insects or by rubbing infected sap on to the leaves of susceptible plants.

Figure 1.3 A tobacco plant showing symptoms of tobacco mosaic disease

Human immunodeficiency virus

Human immunodeficiency virus (HIV), the cause of acquired immune deficiency syndrome (AIDS), is a single-stranded RNA virus. Each HIV particle is more or less spherical in shape and about 0.1 μm in diameter. It has an envelope composed of a lipid membrane, which is taken from the membrane surrounding the host cell. The membrane is studded with particles of glycoproteins (sugars and proteins). The genetic material is enclosed within a hollow capsid made of protein. Along with the genetic material are some molecules of an enzyme called **reverse transcriptase**, which the virus uses to multiply itself.

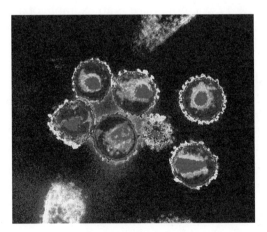

Figure 1.4 Human immunodeficiency viruses (HIV)

HIV is a member of a family of viruses known as **retroviruses**. These viruses are so named because they reverse what seems to be the normal flow of genetic information: from the DNA of a gene to messenger RNA and then to a sequence of amino acids in protein synthesis. When retroviruses multiply, reverse transcriptase is used to make copies of DNA from their viral RNA. The viral DNA, known as a provirus, is then spliced into the host cell's own DNA in an act of piracy, so that the host cell is now equipped to make copies of the virus. Details of the life-cycle of HIV are described in Chapter 9.

Bacteriophages

The term 'bacteriophage' means 'bacteria eater'. Bacteriophages are viruses that infect bacterial cells. Probably the best known is the T2 bacteriophage. It is a parasite of the colon bacterium *Escherichia coli*.

Structure of the T2 bacteriophage

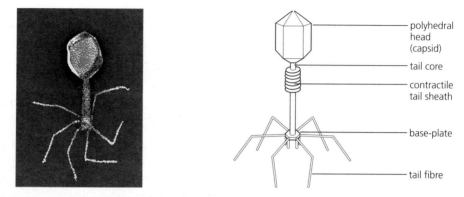

polyhedral head (capsid)

tail core

contractile tail sheath

base-plate

tail fibre

Figure 1.5 A T2 bacteriophage with its tail sheath triggered into contraction in response to contact with specific receptors on the surface of a bacterium

The T2 bacteriophage is an example of a double-stranded DNA virus. It is shaped like a tadpole. It has a broad **head** and a narrow **tail**. The head or capsid encloses a thread-like **DNA molecule**. The tail consists of a sheath surrounding a hollow needle-like **tail core**. A hexagonal **base-plate** bearing six **tail fibres** is attached to the distal end of the tail.

Life-cycle of a T2 bacteriophage

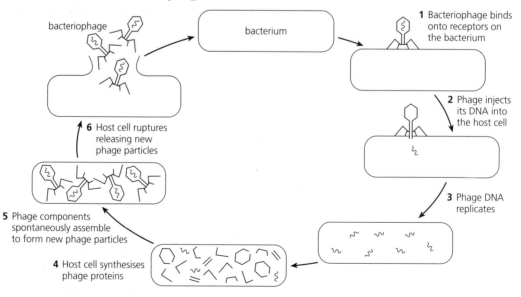

bacteriophage

bacterium

1 Bacteriophage binds onto receptors on the bacterium

2 Phage injects its DNA into the host cell

3 Phage DNA replicates

6 Host cell ruptures releasing new phage particles

5 Phage components spontaneously assemble to form new phage particles

4 Host cell synthesises phage proteins

Figure 1.6 Life-cycle of a T2 bacteriophage

Infection begins when a T2 bacteriophage randomly collides with a colon bacterium and its tail structures bind specifically to receptors on the surface of the bacterium. The attachment triggers the contraction of the tail sheath and the puncturing of the bacterial cell wall by the needle-like tail core. This is followed by injection of the thread-like viral DNA molecule into the host cell. Once inside, the viral DNA directs the host cell's biosynthetic machinery to make component parts of the virus such as the head, tail, tail fibres etc. These parts then spontaneously assemble to form new bacteriophage particles. About 30 minutes after infection, the host cell bursts releasing about 200 replicas of the original virus.

Lambda (λ) virus

The lambda virus is another much studied bacteriophage. It is a double-stranded DNA virus. It uses the K12 strain of the colon bacterium as its host. Like the T2 bacteriophage, it is tadpole-like in appearance. It has a 20-sided head and a flexible, non-contractile tail but lacks tail fibres. Its life-cycle is similar to that of the T2 bacteriophage.

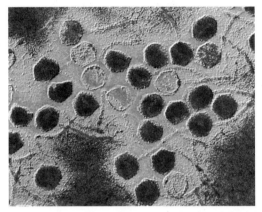

Figure 1.7 An electron micrograph of lambda viruses within the cytoplasm of *E. coli* (× 18 000)

Questions

1 What two parts are common to all viruses?
2 What is i) a retrovirus and ii) a provirus?
3 Describe the life cycle of a **named** virus.

Prokaryotae (bacterial kingdom)

The prokaryotes are unicellular or filamentous organisms consisting of cells that lack a membrane-bound nucleus and membrane-bound organelles. They comprise mainly bacteria and cyanobacteria (formerly known as blue–green algae).

Bacteria are probably the most widely distributed organisms on Earth. They are present in the soil, in the air, on mountain tops, in the depths of the deepest oceans, in the food we eat, in the water we drink and within our bodies. Bacteria are especially abundant in warm, moist places that are rich in organic matter.

Bacteria are smaller than plant or animal cells but much larger than viruses. The vast majority are between 0.5 and 1.0 μm wide and between 1 and 5 μm long.

Classification of bacteria

By shape

1 bacilli (rod-shaped)

streptobacilli (chains)

2 cocci (spherical)

diplococci (pairs)

streptococci (chains)

staphylococci (bunches)

3 spirilla (cork-screw-shaped)

4 spirochaetes (thin, long, cork-screw-shaped)

5 vibrios (comma-shaped)

Figure 1.8 Classification of bacteria based on their shape

Bacteria are traditionally classified on the basis of their shape into five groups. These are:

1 **bacilli** (singular: **bacillus**) – rod-shaped
2 **cocci** (singular: **coccus**) – spherical or oval-shaped
3 **spirilla** (singular: **spirillum**) – corkscrew-shaped rods
4 **spirochaetes** – corkscrew-shaped but with long, thin, flexible bodies
5 **vibrios** – comma-shaped.

The prefix 'diplo' may be used to indicate that the bacteria normally exist in pairs, for example **diplococci**. The prefix 'strepto' indicates that the bacteria normally stick together to form chains, for example **streptobacilli**. Bacteria that stick together to form grape-like bunches have the prefix 'staphylo' added to their name, for example **staphylococci**.

By Gram's staining technique

In 1884, a Danish physician named Hans Christian Gram developed a staining technique that is widely used to classify bacteria into two major groups, each comprising a wide variety of different species. Those that stain purple after treatment with Gram's stain are said to be **Gram-positive** whereas those that stain pink are **Gram-negative**.

Gram's staining technique involves first heat-fixing the bacteria on to a clean glass slide. The bacteria are then stained with crystal violet followed by dilute iodine solution. The excess stain is then washed away with a 50 : 50 mixture of acetone alcohol. Gram negative bacteria are decolorised by the acetone–alcohol but Gram-positive bacteria retain the deep-purple colour of crystal violet. Finally, a red dye called safranin is used to counterstain the Gram-negative bacteria pink.

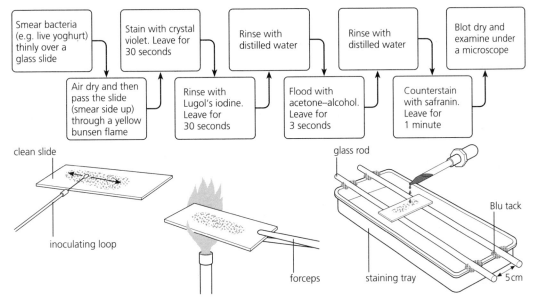

Figure 1.9 The procedure for staining bacteria with Gram stain

Differences in the cell wall structure of the two types of bacteria account for their different reactions to Gram's stain. Gram-positive bacteria have cell walls made largely of **peptidoglycans** (giant molecules of amino sugars and peptides). Crystal violet forms purple complexes with iodine that remain lodged within the spaces of these giant, net-like molecules even after irrigation with acetone–alcohol. Gram-negative bacteria, on the other hand, have a relatively impermeable outer membrane overlying their cell wall. The purple dye is consequently washed off by treatment with acetone–alcohol leaving these bacteria translucent. The counterstain simply makes them more visible.

The Gram reaction is quite useful because Gram-positive bacteria tend to be particularly sensitive to antibiotics such as penicillin and drugs such as sulphonamides; whereas the rigid, relatively impermeable outer membrane of Gram-negative bacteria acts like a shield, which prevents antibiotics and other drugs from combating infection by these bacteria.

Structure of a bacterium

When you view bacteria with a light microscope, they appear to be no more than tiny specks of living matter. With the much higher resolution of an electron microscope, however, it becomes clear that bacteria have a definite internal architecture as shown in Figure 1.11.

7

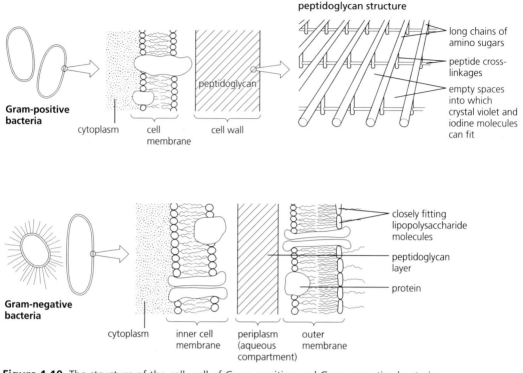

Figure 1.10 The structure of the cell wall of Gram-positive and Gram-negative bacteria

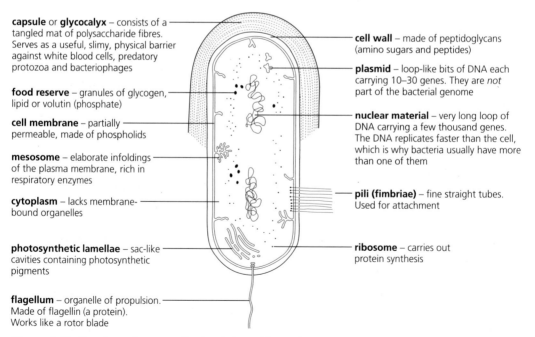

capsule or **glycocalyx** – consists of a tangled mat of polysaccharide fibres. Serves as a useful, slimy, physical barrier against white blood cells, predatory protozoa and bacteriophages

food reserve – granules of glycogen, lipid or volutin (phosphate)

cell membrane – partially permeable, made of phospholids

mesosome – elaborate infoldings of the plasma membrane, rich in respiratory enzymes

cytoplasm – lacks membrane-bound organelles

photosynthetic lamellae – sac-like cavities containing photosynthetic pigments

flagellum – organelle of propulsion. Made of flagellin (a protein). Works like a rotor blade

cell wall – made of peptidoglycans (amino sugars and peptides)

plasmid – loop-like bits of DNA each carrying 10–30 genes. They are *not* part of the bacterial genome

nuclear material – very long loop of DNA carrying a few thousand genes. The DNA replicates faster than the cell, which is why bacteria usually have more than one of them

pili (fimbriae) – fine straight tubes. Used for attachment

ribosome – carries out protein synthesis

Figure 1.11 Structure of a generalised rod-shaped bacterium

Prokaryotic and eukaryotic cells

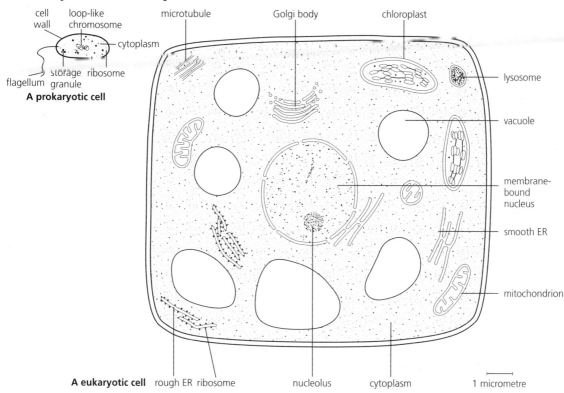

Figure 1.12 Two fundamentally different types of cell

Bacterial cells differ from plant and animal cells in three main ways.

The first and most obvious difference is that bacterial cells are substantially smaller than plant or animal cells. In linear dimensions, plant and animal cells are, on average, 10 times larger than bacterial cells or about 1000 times greater in volume.

Secondly, bacterial cells lack a membrane-bound nucleus, whereas the presence of a rounded, membrane-enveloped nucleus is one of the more distinctive features of plant and animal cells.

Thirdly, bacterial cells lack membrane-bound organelles, such as mitochondria, chloroplasts, Golgi bodies, lysosomes, and endoplasmic reticulum (ER), whereas the presence of these organelles is another characteristic feature of plant and animal cell architecture.

These differences led to the recognition that there are two main types of cells – **prokaryotic** and **eukaryotic** cells. The term 'eukaryotic' was coined from two Greek words: *eu* meaning 'good' or 'true' and *karyon* meaning 'kernel' or 'nut'. It was chosen to emphasise the fact that the eukaryotic cells possess a membrane-bound nucleus. The prefix *pro* means 'in front of' or 'before' and was used to imply that the prokaryotic cells evolved before the eukaryotic cells. The table below summarises the main differences between prokaryotic and eukaryotic cells.

Differences between prokaryotic and eukaryotic cells

Feature	Prokaryotic cell e.g. bacterial cells	Eukaryotic cell e.g. plant and animal cells
Size	About 1 μm^3	About 1000 μm^3
Genetic material	Single loop-like chromosome, not enclosed within a nuclear membrane	More than one thread-like chromosome, enclosed within a nuclear membrane when the cell is not dividing
Chloroplasts	Absent	Present in plant cells, absent in animal cells
Membrane-bound organelles	Absent	Present
Microtubules	Absent	Present
Ribosomes	Smaller (70 S), found scattered in the cytoplasm (S = Svedberg unit, a sedimentation coefficient)	Larger (80 S), often found attached to the endoplasmic reticulum
Flagella	Thin, made of a protein called flagellin. Powered by protons	Thick, made of a sheaf of microtubules. Powered by ATP
Asexual reproduction	By binary fission	By mitosis

Bacterial nutrition

From a nutritional point of view, bacteria can be subdivided into two major groups – those that can utilise carbon dioxide as their sole source of carbon for synthesising their organic food molecules (**autotrophs**) and those that can't (**heterotrophs**).

Autotrophic bacteria

Autotrophic bacteria use carbon dioxide as their sole source of carbon. There are two main types – **photosynthetic** and **chemosynthetic**. Photosynthetic bacteria (e.g. green sulphur bacteria) synthesise their organic food molecules using energy derived from sunlight:

$$2H_2S + CO_2 \underset{\text{energy}}{\overset{\text{light}}{\Rightarrow}} \underset{\text{carbohydrate}}{(CH_2O)} + 2S + H_2O$$

Chemosynthetic bacteria (e.g. nitrifying soil bacteria) derive their energy by oxidation of inorganic molecules:

$$2NH_4^+ + 3O_2 \Rightarrow 2NO_2^- + 2H_2O + 4H^+ (+ \text{energy})$$

ammonium ions   nitrite

Heterotrophic bacteria

Heterotrophic bacteria cannot make use of carbon dioxide as a raw material for synthesising complex organic compounds. They need a supply of ready-made organic molecules (e.g. glucose) to meet their requirements for carbon and energy. The vast

10

majority of heterotrophic bacteria feed as **saprobionts** by secreting digestive enzymes on to organic matter and then absorbing the soluble products of external digestion. Some invade other living organisms to feed as **parasites**.

Bacterial respiration

Bacteria can be divided into three groups depending on their response to molecular oxygen. One group, known as **obligate aerobes**, need free molecular oxygen for their metabolism and growth. Another group, known as **obligate anaerobes**, need oxygen-free environments and are killed even by the briefest exposure to free molecular oxygen. The third group, known as **facultative anaerobes**, can switch from an aerobic mode of life when free molecular oxygen is available, to an anaerobic mode of life should the oxygen supply run out.

All cells, in the presence of oxygen, produce hydrogen peroxide and superoxide (unstable charged atoms of oxygen) as by-products of cell metabolism. The aerobes and facultative anaerobes have enzymes capable of eliminating these harmful substances. Obligate anaerobes lack these protective enzymes.

Endospore formation

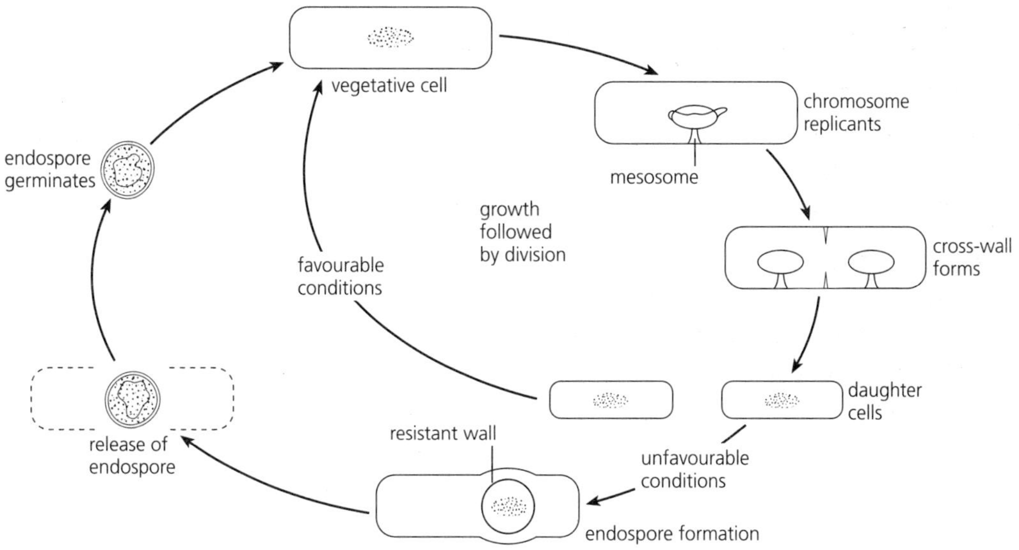

Figure 1.13 The life-cycle of a rod-shaped bacterium

When conditions are unfavourable for growth, for example when food runs out, bacilli are capable of changing into dormant structures known as **endospores**. During endospore formation, the cell loses most of its water, leaving its proteins in a dehydrated state. It also lays down a thick resistant wall around itself. Bacterial endospores can survive boiling at normal pressures for several hours. They are unaffected by acids, alkalis and disinfectants, and they can withstand prolonged periods of freezing or extreme dryness. Wet heat above 120 °C or dry heat in excess of 180 °C kills them.

Asexual reproduction

Under favourable conditions, bacteria reproduce by a process of asexual reproduction known as **binary fission**. The bacterial chromosome replicates and, while this is taking place, the chromosome may be held in position by attachment to the cell membrane. An in-growth of the cell membrane forms transversely across the cell followed by the laying down of a new cell wall, which divides the cell into two. If conditions are favourable, bacteria feed, grow to full size and then divide and repeat this process of binary fission every 10 to 60 minutes.

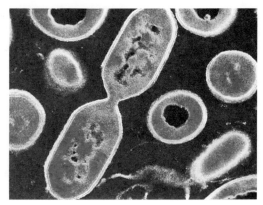

Figure 1.14 A bacterium dividing by binary fission (× 22 000)

Ways by which bacteria acquire new pieces of genetic information

There are three ways by which bacteria can acquire new genetic material, by:

- **transduction**
- **transformation**
- **conjugation**.

Transduction

Bacteriophages can sometimes pick up a fragment of bacterial DNA and transfer it to other bacterial cells as shown in Figure 1.15a. This natural method of interbacterial transfer of genes is known as transduction.

Transformation

In transformation, DNA released into the environment by cell death or other natural process may simply enter a living bacterial cell by penetrating the cell wall and the cell membrane. For example, suspension in cold calcium chloride solution followed by brief heat-shock will cause bacteria to take up laboratory purified DNA from their surroundings; precisely why this technique works is not clear.

Conjugation

Bacteria that possess what are called 'F factor' genes are capable of exhibiting a primitive form of sexuality known as conjugation. These genes are carried on small circular bits of DNA known as **plasmids.**

Most bacteria carry plasmids, often several of them. These plasmids exist alongside the bacterial chromosome and are capable of replicating independently of the bacterial chromosome. The F factor genes, which some of them carry, code for certain proteins needed for conjugation. During conjugation, a fine, straight tubular appendage known as a **conjugation tube** forms, which physically connects the two

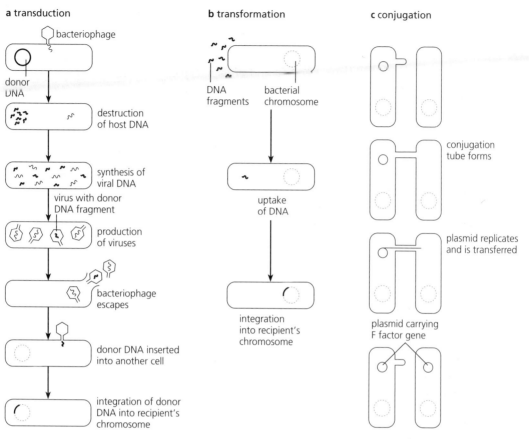

a transduction

bacteriophage

donor DNA

destruction of host DNA

synthesis of viral DNA

virus with donor DNA fragment

production of viruses

bacteriophage escapes

donor DNA inserted into another cell

integration of donor DNA into recipient's chromosome

b transformation

DNA fragments   bacterial chromosome

uptake of DNA

integration into recipient's chromosome

c conjugation

conjugation tube forms

plasmid replicates and is transferred

plasmid carrying F factor gene

Figure 1.15 **a** Transduction; **b** Transformation; **c** Conjugation

bacteria. The circular plasmid replicates and the newly synthesised linear strand of DNA passes through the connecting tube from one bacterium (donor) to the other (recipient). In this way, plasmids promote their own transfer from one bacterial cell to another. Since some larger plasmids carry up to about 100 genes, the recipient cell can, by conjugation, receive quite a substantial package of new genetic information. Conjugations can occur between bacteria that are not of the same species.

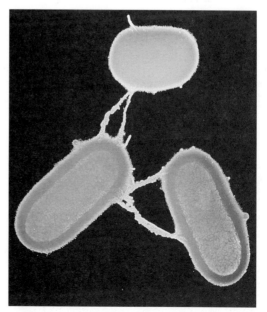

Figure 1.16 Conjugating bacteria (× 14 000)

Questions

4 Make a large labelled drawing to illustrate the structure of a prokaryotic cell.
5 List the similarities and the differences between prokaryotic and eukaryotic cells.
6 Describe endospore formation in bacteria and explain its biological significance.
7 What are plasmids and in what ways are they similar to viruses?
8 Describe how Gram's stain is used to distinguish between Gram-positive and Gram-negative bacteria.

Protoctista

Protoctists are eukaryotic organisms that were traditionally classified as algae and protozoa (single-celled animals) but have since been regrouped into a kingdom of their own. The Kingdom Protoctista comprises mostly unicellular but some multicellular organisms that differ from plants or animals in one major way – they do not exhibit embryonic development. A protoctist of special interest to microbiologists is the unicellular green alga called *Chlorella*.

Chlorella

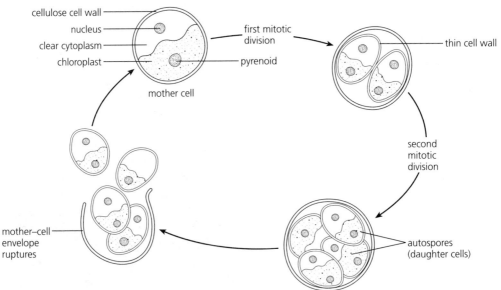

Figure 1.17 Structure and life-cycle of *Chlorella*

Chlorella is a non-motile, unicellular green alga that occurs in freshwater ponds, canals, moist soil and lakes. The individual cells are spherical and about 7 μm in diameter. Each cell possesses a grass-green, somewhat cup-shaped **chloroplast**. A small protein body known as a **pyrenoid** exists within the chloroplast. The pyrenoid consists largely of an enzyme that acts by catalysing the capture of carbon dioxide molecules for photosynthesis. *Chlorella* reproduces asexually by the formation of **autospores** as shown in Figure 1.17. It is the fastest growing single-celled alga and is easy to culture. *Chlorella* is widely used in scientific research.

Paramecium

Another very common freshwater protoctist is a protozoan called *Paramecium*. It is almost invariably encountered when a drop of pond water containing some decaying plant matter is examined under a microscope. *Paramecium* belongs to a large group of unicellular microorganisms that, without exception, possess **cilia** – tiny, whip-like structures that project from the surface of the cell. These organisms have been classified together into a phylum called the Ciliophora (ciliates). Some ciliates possess a few cilia; others, like *Paramecium*, have a body covered with cilia. The cilia beat rhythmically and have a locomotory or food-gathering function.

Paramecium feeds on bacteria and particles of organic matter suspended in the water. *Paramecium caudatum* (a common species) has a slipper-shaped body with an oral groove on the indented slide of its body (Figure 1.18). The oral groove leads to its mouth. The constant beating of cilia around its oral groove draws a current of water containing food particles towards its mouth.

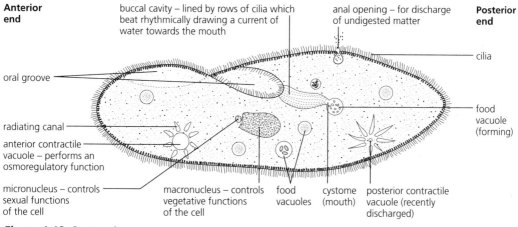

Anterior end — buccal cavity – lined by rows of cilia which beat rhythmically drawing a current of water towards the mouth — anal opening – for discharge of undigested matter — **Posterior end** — cilia

oral groove — food vacuole (forming)

radiating canal

anterior contractile vacuole – performs an osmoregulatory function

micronucleus – controls sexual functions of the cell — macronucleus – controls vegetative functions of the cell — food vacuoles — cystome (mouth) — posterior contractile vacuole (recently discharged)

Figure 1.18 *Paramecium*

From a biotechnological point of view, ciliates play an important role in the sewage treatment industry. They feed on bacteria and other fine organic particles, thus helping to keep bacterial populations in check (see Chapter 6, page 93).

Fungi

Fungi are eukaryotic, spore-bearing organisms that lack chlorophyll and are mostly filamentous but sometimes unicellular. They have cell walls made not of cellulose but mainly of a nitrogen-containing polysaccharide called **chitin**. The majority feed as saprobionts by secreting digestive enzymes on to organic matter and absorbing the soluble products of external digestion.

Some fungi live as parasites by feeding on the living tissues of other organisms. Those that cause disease are known as pathogens. Parasitic fungi cause as much as 75% of infectious plant diseases. Well-known fungal diseases of plants include the mildews, blights, root rots and cankers, rusts and smuts. Fungal diseases of humans include athlete's foot and ringworm.

Some fungi are commercially exploitable. Examples include the yeasts used in the baking and brewing industries and in the industrial manufacture of ethanol. Another fungus of commercial importance is *Penicillium*, some species are used in the manufacture of blue cheeses and others are used in the manufacture of the antibiotic penicillin.

Vegetative structure

The vegetative body of a fungus typically consists of a mat of fine, branching, tubular filaments known as **hyphae**. The entire network of hyphae, that is, the whole vegetative body of a fungus is known as a **mycelium**. Each hypha consists of a single row of cells. The hyphae are said to be **septate** if the cells that make up the hyphae have cross walls. They are said to be **non-septate** if the cells lack cross walls.

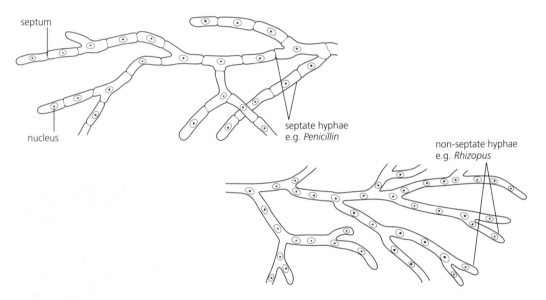

Figure 1.19 Two types of fungal hyphae

Fungal cells have a lining of cytoplasm surrounding a central vacuole, which is filled with a watery cell sap. In non-septate forms, the nuclei are scattered throughout the cytoplasm. In septate forms, the hyphal cells may contain one, two or many nuclei. The cross walls of septate hyphae are perforated by numerous pores or, in some species, by a single pore. The pores allow the fungus to circulate nutrients taken up by invading hyphae. In this way essential nutrients that are in short supply at one microsite may be supplemented by translocation from elsewhere.

Some fungi, notably yeasts, have a body consisting of individual ovoid cells that grow by budding. Others exhibit unicellular as well as filamentous growth phases. The fungus *Mucor rouxii*, for example, develops a mat-like growth of slender filaments under aerobic conditions and a yeast-like growth of single cells under anaerobic conditions. The term 'yeast' is used to refer to fungi that consist of just a few cells or even of just one cell.

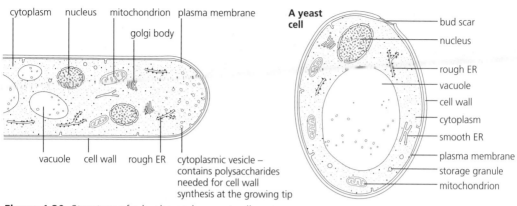

Figure 1.20 Structure of a hypha and a yeast cell

Baker's and Brewer's yeast

Saccharomyces cerevisiae, the common baker's and brewer's yeast, is a unicellular fungus of great economic importance. It is used to leaven bread, to prepare beer, wine and other alcoholic drinks, and to produce alcohol for use as a fuel and as a chemical. The cells of *S. cerevisiae* are oval-shaped and between 6 and 8 μm long and about 5 to 6 μm wide.

Asexual reproduction

S. cerevisiae reproduces asexually by **budding**. A small bud develops usually on one side of the parent cell. The nucleus then divides by mitosis to give rise to two daughter nuclei, one of which migrates into the enlarging bud. When the bud reaches a certain size, it separates from the mother cell and may then itself start to bud.

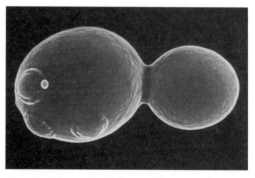

Figure 1.21 Budding yeast cells

Penicillium

Penicillium is a multicellular mould fungus. It is one of the most common types of fungi. Most of the blue moulds seen growing on over-ripe citrus and other fruits belong to the genus *Penicillium*. It has a branched, filamentous body and its hyphae are septate.

Asexual reproduction

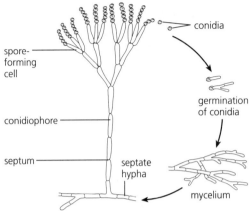

Figure 1.22 Asexual life-cycle of *Penicillium*

Penicillium reproduces by means of spores. When the mycelium has grown to a certain size, it produces long, aerial hyphae called **conidiophores**, which branch to give rise to a cluster of spore-forming cells. From the tips of these cells, naked cytoplasm oozes and rounds off to become spores known as **conidia**. The grey–green colour of the spores is responsible for the colour of the mould fungus.

The black bread mould *Rhizopus* (*Mucor*)

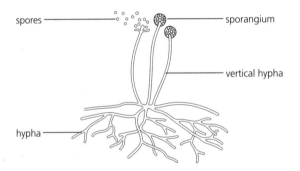

Figure 1.23 *Rhizopus (Mucor)*, a mould fungus

The pin moulds, such as the black bread mould *Rhizopus stolonifer* (previously known as *Mucor stolonifer*), are also common mould fungi. *Rhizopus* has a filamentous body made up of a number of branching, non-septate hyphae. It plays an important role in the decomposition of plant remains on the forest floor.

Questions

9 List the similarities and the differences between fungal hyphae and yeast cells.
10 Give an illustrated account of the process of asexual reproduction in *Chlorella*.
11 Tabulate the differences between a bacterial cell and a unicellular alga like *Chlorella*.
12 List four ways in which humans make use of yeast.

Examination questions

1 The diagrams show some of the stages in the life-cycle of a virus which attacks a bacterium. Use information from the diagrams to help answer the questions which follow.

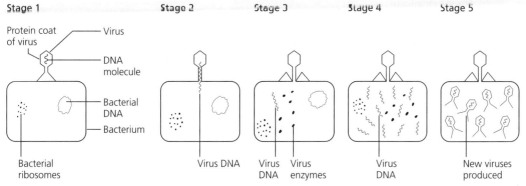

Stage 1   Stage 2   Stage 3   Stage 4   Stage 5

a i) Suggest the purpose of the original strand of DNA injected into the bacterium by the virus.
ii) Suggest how the virus DNA carries out this function. (4)
b What appear to be the functions of the enzymes formed by the virus? Suggest their importance in the life-cycle of the virus. (4)
c Stage 4 shows the presence of many more molecules of DNA. State how they have been produced. (2)
d What evidence in the diagrams helped to show that DNA rather than protein was the chemical nature of a gene? (2)

(total = 12)
WJEC, June 1986

2 a The bacterial cell shown in the photograph [below] is one micrometre (µm) in length while the plant cell is 10 micrometres (10 µm) in length. Assuming that the cells are perfect cylinders, their relative volumes will be approximately

1 : 6   1 : 60   1 : 600   1 : 6000

Ring the correct answer.

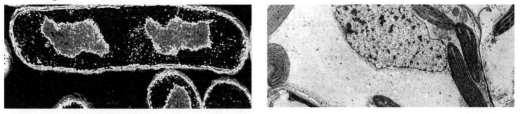

b Cells of the bacterial type are termed *prokaryotic*. What is the corresponding term for the other type of cell shown and for other similar cells?
c On the plant cell photograph, arrow and label
 – a chloroplast,
 – the cytoplasmic membrane,
 – a mitochondrion,
 – a desmosome (plasmodesma).

d Other than the differences in size, pick out what you consider to be the most important difference between the two cells shown in regard to
  i) their genetic material
  ii) their cytoplasm.
e Suggest a part of the plant from which the cell shown might have been taken.

(total = 9)

O & C, June 1982

3 The Human Immunodeficiency Virus (HIV) believed to be responsible for AIDS is thought to have a structure shown below.

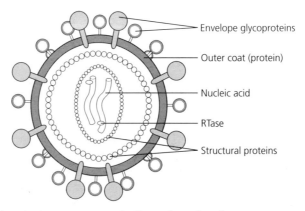

a Which **two** biochemical components, indicated on the diagram, are generally common to all viruses? (2)
b The virus shown may be described as a *non-cellular pathogen*. Explain the meaning of this phrase. (2)
c Suggest two ways in which this virus differs from a bacteriophage. (2)
d In the table below give **three** differences between viruses and bacteria. (3)

Viruses	Bacteria

(total = 9)

UODLE, Dec 1994

Suggestions for learning experiences

Activity 25.7 Growth of *Chlorella* in 'eutrophic conditions' (Investigation). *Advanced Biology Study Guide*, CG Clegg and DG Mackean with PH Openshaw and RC Reynolds. John Murray (Publishers) Ltd 1996, page 290.

Activity 25.11 *Mucor* as a coprophilous fungus (Demonstration/Investigation). *Advanced Biology Study Guide*, CG Clegg and DG Mackean with PH Openshaw and RC Reynolds. John Murray (Publishers) Ltd 1996, page 294.

General safety precautions

In warm, moist conditions and when supplied with an abundance of nutrients, microorganisms multiply rapidly. A few harmful bacteria can become many millions of disease-causing microorganisms within a few hours. It is therefore very important to observe strict rules of cleanliness and good laboratory practices when working with microorganisms.

- Hands should be thoroughly washed with soap and warm water at the start of a microbiological practical and again before leaving the laboratory.
- Always treat microbial cultures as if they contain disease-causing microorganisms.
- Use laboratory overalls to protect your clothing from contamination and becoming a source of infection for spreading disease outside the laboratory.
- Avoid eating, drinking or any hand to mouth actions including licking labels, sucking pens or mouth pipetting.
- Avoid breathing on to a nutrient agar plate when its lid is off.
- Cultures should be examined in their unopened containers.
- Disinfect your laboratory working area with a paper towel dipped in a **clear** phenolic disinfectant (e.g. Clearsol, Hycolin, Stericol, etc.) at the start and at again at the end of a laboratory practical. (Most **cloudy** phenols and saponated cresols, for example Lysol, are toxic and corrosive and may not kill bacterial spores, and should not be used.)
- Spilled cultures should be covered with towels or a cloth soaked in a suitable, freshly prepared disinfectant and left for at least 15 minutes before being mopped up. Disposable gloves should be worn and the mopped up material should be placed in an autoclavable plastic bag for autoclaving before disposal. Contaminated skin should be washed with soap and hot water.
- After use, all instruments, glassware, etc., should be placed in a vessel containing a suitable disinfectant.
- For reasons of safety, schools should culture only specific microorganisms obtained from recognised suppliers as listed in *Microbiology: An HMI Guide for Schools and non-advanced Further Education* (ISBN 0 11 270578 2) and in *Safety in Science Education*, a DfEE publication (ISBN 0 11 270915 X) obtainable from HMSO. Soil cultures carry pathogenic bacteria such as *Clostridium tetani,* and the subculture of environmental microorganisms as described in the text (although a routine procedure for industrial microbiologists) is not permitted at the school level.

The cultivation of microorganisms

Many microorganisms can be cultured successfully in the laboratory if they are provided with a watery solution containing nutrients, access to oxygen (if they are aerobic), a suitable temperature, optimal pH conditions, an absence of harmful chemicals and, finally, space to grow and reproduce with minimal competition from other organisms. The exceptions include viruses and obligate parasites.

Need for water

Although many types of microorganisms live on land, they are all essentially water organisms in the sense that the microhabitat in which they feed and grow is watery; some fungal hyphae grow in damp air. To culture microorganisms in the laboratory, it is necessary, therefore, to recreate their watery environment by providing them with a water-based culture medium. The water may be in liquid form, such as a broth or soup, or it may be bound within the intermolecular spaces of a jelly-like solid. Water makes up about 95% of the total weight of most bacteria and fungi. The vegetative phases of these organisms will not grow in the absence of water.

Nutritional requirements

The culture medium must also supply all the nutritive requirements of the microorganisms. Bacteria, fungi and protoctists need a **source of carbon** and a **source of energy**. For heterotrophic bacteria and fungi, this could take the form of a carbohydrate like glucose. The carbohydrate would also supply the **hydrogen** and **oxygen** needed for the synthesis of most organic compounds.

Another essential element is **nitrogen**. Many types of bacteria and fungi can make use of an inorganic source of nitrogen, for example **ammonium ions** (NH_4^+) or **nitrates** (NO_3^-). Others require their nitrogen in the form of complex organic compounds such as **amino acids** or **peptides**. Other essential elements, including phosphorus, sulphur, sodium, potassium, calcium, magnesium, iron and traces of manganese, cobalt, copper, molybdenum and zinc, are generally supplied in the form of **dissolved mineral salts**.

Some types of bacteria cannot synthesise certain vitamins (usually vitamins of the B complex) and need to be provided with these so-called **growth factors**.

Nowadays, most media for the laboratory culture of microorganisms are prepared from tablets purchased from commercial suppliers. If these are not available, a balanced chemical fertiliser (the type used by gardeners), together with a little sugar dissolved in water, will support the growth of many types of bacteria and fungi.

Oxygen supply

If aerobic microorganisms are cultured in a liquid medium, they will (except near the surface of the liquid) rapidly use up the available dissolved oxygen. The usual procedure for supplying oxygen to microorganisms growing in a liquid culture is to aerate the liquid by bubbling filtered air through it.

Suitable temperature

Another condition for the successful culture of microorganisms is a suitable temperature. Low temperatures (below 5 °C) generally inhibit growth because enzymatic reactions proceed much too slowly. On the other extreme, temperatures above 80 °C kill even the heat-loving microbes (known as **thermophiles**). For optimum growth, bacterial cultures should generally be incubated at 30–37 °C. Fungal cultures grow better at slightly lower temperatures, generally between 25 and 27 °C).

Optimal pH

The pH of a culture medium is important because most microorganisms will grow only within a particular range of pH. The pH of a medium affects the activity of microbial (and other) enzymes. Fungi generally prefer slightly acidic conditions (pH 5–6) whereas most bacteria grow best in neutral conditions (pH 7).

Elimination of competitors – aseptic techniques

This involves adopting a variety of procedures collectively known as **aseptic techniques.** They are designed to exclude unwanted microorganisms from a particular environment. In its most basic form, it consists of **sterilising** all glassware, instruments, nutrient media, etc. before using them for culturing microorganisms.

Sterilisation by pressure cooking

Sterilisation is usually done by using either a domestic **pressure cooker** or a large, specially designed, steam-filled pressure cooker known as an **autoclave**. The pressure of steam within the pressure cooker builds up to 103 kN m^{-2}, which raises the boiling point of water to 121 °C. An exposure of 15–20 minutes to heated steam of this temperature kills even the most heat-resistant bacterial endospores. Dry heat is less efficient and equipment will need to be kept in an oven set at 180 °C for three hours if they are to be properly sterilised.

To use a pressure cooker as a laboratory steriliser, water is placed in the bottom of the pressure cooker to a depth of 1 cm. The items to be sterilised are then loaded into the pressure cooker. Screw-capped McCartney bottles containing nutrient agar should have their caps loosely screwed on. Flasks or tubes used as containers for nutrient broth should be stoppered with cotton-wool plugs. The plugs should be wrapped on the outside with aluminium foil to keep them dry during autoclaving. A strip of autoclave indicator tape may be used to secure the piece of foil in place. Markings on the indicator tape develop into a dark colour if the pressure-cooking procedure is satisfactory. Finally, the lid should be firmly fixed into position with the valve open.

The pressure cooker is heated to boil the water; only when steam is emerging freely through the open valve (indicating that the air within has been driven out) should the valve be shut by using the weight. Maximum pressure is maintained for 20 minutes by controlling the heat supply. The heat is then turned off and the pressure cooker left to cool in the room. To avoid creating suction, the weight should not be removed until the pressure within the pressure cooker has returned to zero. Unless required for immediate use, the screw caps for the McCartney bottles should be tightly screwed on to prevent contamination of the sterilised medium.

Killing by flaming

Another standard aseptic technique is sterilisation by flaming the working surface of instruments, for example inoculating loops, forceps and the rims of vessels used for dispensing sterile media. The heat of the flame not only kills microbes but it also creates rising hot-air currents, which carry away microbes that would otherwise fall into the open culture vessel. Figure 2.1 illustrates the techniques for flaming.

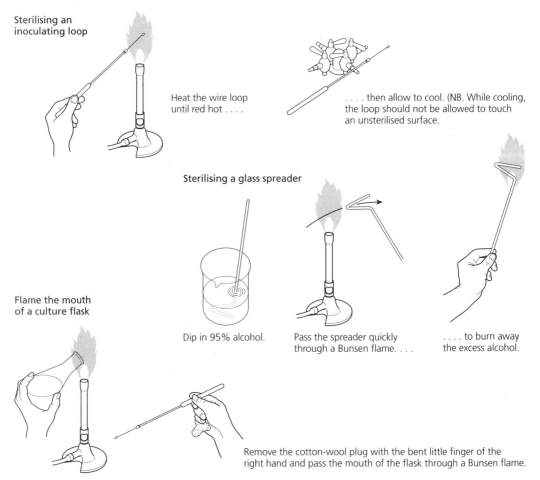

Sterilising an inoculating loop

Heat the wire loop until red hot . . . .

. . . . then allow to cool. (NB. While cooling, the loop should not be allowed to touch an unsterilised surface.

Sterilising a glass spreader

Flame the mouth of a culture flask

Dip in 95% alcohol.

Pass the spreader quickly through a Bunsen flame. . . .

. . . . to burn away the excess alcohol.

Remove the cotton-wool plug with the bent little finger of the right hand and pass the mouth of the flask through a Bunsen flame.

Figure 2.1 Aseptic techniques – killing by flaming

A major cause of contamination in laboratories is **microbial aerosol formation**. These are fine droplets of water containing live bacteria or spores that are released into the air. Aerosols can form when wire loops carrying a culture splutter during flaming. To reduce this hazard, the loop should be introduced into a flame slowly. Aerosols can also form when a spilt liquid splashes on to the ground.

Prevention of entry of contaminants

Covered sterile transparent dishes (known as Petri dishes) containing sterile nutrients set in agar are generally used to provide a protected environment for microorganisms to grow. Flasks or tubes stoppered with cotton-wool plugs can also be used. To prevent entry of unwanted contaminants, like airborne spores, the lids of the Petri dishes should be opened only just enough and for as short a time as possible whenever it is necessary to open them.

Sterilisation by filtration

High-efficiency particulate air (HEPA) filters are used to screen microorganisms from the air before it is bubbled through the liquid medium. The filters, normally made of paper, have maximum pore sizes that are smaller than bacterial cells. Standard bacteriological filters have pore diameters of 0.45 μm.

Sterile laboratory conditions

Examples of further measures that can be taken to reduce the risk of contamination by unwanted microorganisms are swabbing laboratory working surfaces with a suitable disinfectant; washing hands with soap and water at the start and at the end of a laboratory working session; not breathing over microbial cultures; properly disposing of cultures; keeping laboratories draught-free.

Plating out the medium

A boiling water-bath is used to melt solidified sterile nutrient agar. Solidified agar melts at 98 °C and stays liquid until it cools to 38 °C. The melted agar is ready for pouring when the bottle can be held comfortably in the palm of the hand (45–50 °C). The actual process of pouring is critical, because airborne spores could enter to contaminate the medium. To reduce this risk, plating should be carried out in a draught-free room and the lid of the sterile Petri dish should be opened only just enough to allow entry of the mouth of the bottle. The lid should then be quickly replaced and the dish given a gentle swirl to ensure even distribution of the medium.

Enrichment cultivation

The isolation of microorganisms from a natural habitat like the soil usually requires a preliminary step called **enrichment cultivation** (see note on safety on page 21). For soil bacteria, this consists of infecting a tube or flask of sterile nutrient broth with a few grains of fresh garden soil. There are thousands of bacteria on those few grains of soil, and if the tube or flask is incubated at 30–35 °C the medium will soon be teeming with a variety of soil bacteria (some of which could be pathogenic). The next step is to inoculate a tiny drop of the culture on to the surface of a sterile plate of nutrient agar by a procedure known as **streaking**.

Streak plating

The ideal tool for streaking a plate of nutrient agar is an **inoculating loop**. It consists of a length of nichrome wire inserted into a metal or wooden handle with its free end shaped to form a small loop. The wire and its loop are heated till red-hot in a Bunsen flame to sterilise them. The loop is then left to cool before being dipped into the broth to pick up a drop of the bacterial culture. A series of streaks is then made across the plate with the loop held almost horizontal to avoid digging into the agar. Streaking in a zigzag pattern is a fairly popular technique.

Preparing a pure culture from a mixed culture of bacteria

The easiest way of obtaining a pure culture, that is one consisting of just one type of bacteria, from a mixture of bacteria is to use a technique known as the **quadrant streak method**. It is based on the principle that bacteria cannot move very much on the surface of solidified agar and that, if the inoculum is spread thinly enough, each separated individual will grow and multiply (where it fell from the inoculating loop) to form a visible aggregate of similar bacteria called a **colony**.

An inoculating loop is put in a Bunsen flame till red-hot to sterilise it. The cooled loop is then dipped into the broth containing the mixed culture to pick up a drop of the bacterial culture. The inoculum is placed near the rim of a sterile nutrient agar plate and several parallel streaks are made across that quadrant of the plate. The loop is then flamed and allowed to cool. The plate is turned through 100° and a further series of parallel streaks is made across the previous streaks, as shown in Figure 2.2. The two remaining quadrants are each streaked in the same way using a sterile loop. By the fourth series of streaks, the inoculum will have been so thinly spread out that individual bacteria falling off the loop will have been well spaced out. The plate is then incubated at 30 °C. During incubation, each bacterium multiplies to form a colony of similar individuals. If a portion of one of the pure colonies is removed with a sterile inoculating loop and used as an inoculum to a start a new culture, the new culture will consist of just one type of microbe. (NB. The opening of culture plates is not permitted at the school and non-advanced Further Education level.)

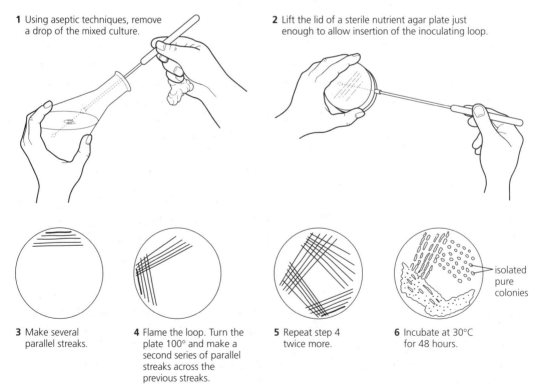

1 Using aseptic techniques, remove a drop of the mixed culture.

2 Lift the lid of a sterile nutrient agar plate just enough to allow insertion of the inoculating loop.

3 Make several parallel streaks.

4 Flame the loop. Turn the plate 100° and make a second series of parallel streaks across the previous streaks.

5 Repeat step 4 twice more.

6 Incubate at 30°C for 48 hours.

isolated pure colonies

Figure 2.2 Preparing a pure culture from a mixed culture of bacteria

Types of culture media

Liquid media

A liquid, nutrient medium is commonly used as a general purpose medium for culturing bacteria. The watery medium provides a suitable physical environment for growth of the microorganisms. In schools, a liquid medium consisting of nutrient broth tablets dissolved in water is commonly used as a general purpose medium for subculturing selected harmless bacteria such as *Bacillus subtilis* or *Escherichia coli* (obtainable from reputable suppliers) for use in school laboratory experiments.

Most large-scale industrial fermenter systems use liquid media. One advantage of this is that it can be mechanically stirred, making it easier to distribute the nutrients evenly and maintain optimum conditions throughout the culture medium. Another advantage is that sterile filtered air can be pumped through a liquid medium, thereby making it possible for aerobic microorganisms to be cultured on a large scale submerged in a tank filled with liquid. Provided strict aseptic procedures are adopted, samples can be readily withdrawn from a liquid medium in order to monitor the progress of the culture. Nutrients and other substances can also be added easily from time to time to adjust the composition of the liquid medium. Cells in a liquid medium cannot, however, be kept isolated from one another, and if the aim is to obtain isolated colonies from a mixed culture (consisting of different types of microorganisms) a liquid medium is clearly not suitable. There are also some types of fungi that cannot be cultured on liquid media.

Solid media

The main advantage of using solid media is that they allow physical separation of individual cells. The separated individuals will then multiply within a small area to form isolated colonies from which pure cultures can be obtained. Solid media are used to culture those species of filamentous fungi and yeasts that will only grow on low-moisture substrates. Solid media may also be used to culture fastidious species that require special nutrients and that need the physical protection of a solid medium against competition from hardier species.

One disadvantage of using solid media is that aerobic species will need to confine themselves to growing near the surface of the medium. For large-scale culture of aerobic microorganisms on solid media, several shallow pans are needed – a much more cumbersome method when compared with submerged culture within a large, liquid-filled tank. Also, compared with a liquid medium, it is more difficult to withdraw samples.

Selective media

During the preliminary enrichment stage for the isolation of bacteria, selective media are often used to promote the growth of some bacteria while inhibiting the growth of others. For example, if the aim is to encourage the growth of free-living nitrogen-fixing bacteria from the soil, the culture medium chosen would contain sugars and minerals but lack a source of nitrogen by leaving out ammonium salts. Only nitrogen-fixers, which can use atmospheric nitrogen to form ammonium ions, would be able to grow in such a medium. When plated out, the colonies that develop would consist mostly of nitrogen-fixers. In time, of course, the nitrogen-fixers would release ammonium ions into the medium and a mixed culture would develop. Similarly, a selective medium containing sulphur in place of glucose would favour the growth of sulphur bacteria.

If, instead of altering the composition of the nutrients, the pH of the medium was altered by adding a weak acid, the growth of fungi would be favoured. Fungi prefer a slightly acidic medium whereas most bacteria prefer one that is neutral.

Many types of selective media contain **inhibitors** to suppress the growth of contaminants. A special formulation called MacConkey's agar, for example, contains 0.5% sodium taurocholate, a bile salt, to suppress the growth of Gram-positive bacteria.

Indicator media

Some media incorporate a pH indicator to provide information about the metabolic activities of the organisms being cultured. MacConkey's agar, for example, is commonly used in hospital laboratories to isolate *Salmonella* from human faeces. *Salmonella* is a genus of pathogenic Gram-negative bacteria responsible for a type of food poisoning. The MacConkey's agar used for culturing bacteria in human faeces contains 1% lactose and a pH indicator (as well as the bile salt mentioned earlier). The indicator turns red if the pH drops to below 6.8.

Escherichia coli and other harmless intestinal bacteria that can ferment lactose, release an acid as an end-product of lactose fermentation. The acid turns the colonies red. *Salmonella*, on the other hand, is a non-lactose-fermenting species and it forms colourless colonies. MacConkey's agar is, therefore, not only a selective medium but also an indicator medium. It inhibits the growth of Gram-positive intestinal bacteria, reveals the harmless Gram-negative bacteria as reddish colonies and identifies the pathogenic Gram-negative bacteria as colourless colonies.

E. coli 0157, the virulent strain responsible for a dangerous form of food poisoning characterised by bloody diarrhoea, is lactose-fermenting, pathogenic and Gram-negative. It is not, however, a normal inhabitant of the human intestine. Its natural home is in the guts of cattle.

Estimating microbial numbers

It is sometimes necessary to report on the population density of microbes in a culture or in drinking water, milk or a food product. There are several ways of doing this and these can be subdivided into direct and indirect methods. The direct methods include **direct counting** and the **measurements of dry mass.** The indirect methods, which measure some property that is proportional to population density, include two commonly used techniques known respectively as **dilution-plating** and **turbidimetry**.

Direct counting

In this method, the number of cells in a known volume of a liquid sample is counted by viewing under a microscope. A specially designed slide, known as a **haemocytometer** (Figure 2.3), is used for counting eukaryotic cells, for example

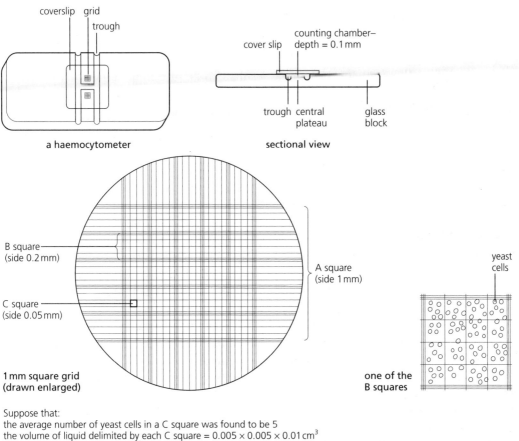

Suppose that:
the average number of yeast cells in a C square was found to be 5
the volume of liquid delimited by each C square = $0.005 \times 0.005 \times 0.01 \, cm^3$
the number of yeast cells in $1 \, cm^3$ of the culture = $5 \times 1 \div 0.005 \times 0.005 \times 0.01$

Figure 2.3 Using a haemocytometer

yeast. (Bacterial cells are counted with a slide of similar design called a
Petroff–Hauser counting chamber.) The haemocytometer has a counting chamber
that can be accurately filled to a depth of 0.1 mm. A grid covering an area $1 \, mm^2$ is
etched on to the slide. The $1 \, mm^2$ grid is subdivided into 25 smaller (B) squares,
each of which is further subdivided into 16 even smaller (C) squares. There are, in
other words, a total of 400 C squares, each $0.0025 \, mm^2$ in area within the $1 \, mm^2$
grid. The volume of liquid over each of the C squares is therefore $0.0025 \times 0.1 =$
$0.00025 \, mm^3$ or $0.00000025 \, cm^3$. From the average number of cells per C square, the
population density per cm^3 of the raw sample can be worked out.

To use the haemocytometer, a drop of the sample is placed on the grid with a
sterile Pasteur pipette. The haemocytometer's special coverslip is then placed on the
slide. When correctly positioned, rainbow markings called Newton's rings should be
visible through those parts of the coverslip that are in contact with the shoulders of
the haemocytometer. The number of cells in several randomly chosen C squares is
counted and averaged and the results are used to calculate the number of cells
per cm^3 of the raw sample.

The main disadvantages of the method are:

- dead cells are sometimes counted together with living cells, leading to inaccuracies
- due to the small volume of the sample results can be unreliable especially if the number of cells actually counted is small
- the presence of debris may sometimes interfere with counting.

The main advantage is that, with experience, counts can be made easily and quickly.

Measurements of dry cell mass

In this method, a measured volume of the sample is spun in a centrifuge to cause the cells to settle to the bottom. The **supernatant liquid** is then decanted and the cells are washed by resuspension in distilled water. This is followed again by centrifugation and the process is repeated at least twice more to remove unassimilated nutrients or waste products. The final resuspension is then transferred into a preweighed vessel and left in an oven set at 90 °C for drying to constant weight. The weight of the vessel is subtracted from the final weight to give the mass of the cells in the sample.

The main objection to this method is that it is time consuming and not very sensitive. Bacteria weigh very little and a large quantity of the culture may need to be sacrificed to gather enough bacteria for weighing. The method is better suited for monitoring the growth of larger microorganisms, such as filamentous fungi.

Dilution-plating

This method is based on the assumption that each viable bacterium, when plated out on to solid nutrient agar, grows by asexual multiplication to become a single colony that can then be counted. In practice, a measured volume of the sample, for example raw milk, is added to a known volume of diluent liquid (usually sterile water). The diluent should not support cell multiplication or cause any loss of cell viability. **Dilution** is usually necessary because the raw sample may contain so many bacteria that, when plated out, the colonies merge making accurate counting impossible.

A series of dilutions are made in the following way, see also Figure 2.4.

1 1 cm^3 of the raw sample is withdrawn with a sterile pipette and added to 9 cm^3 of autoclaved water in a sterile test tube to bring the population density down to 10%.
2 After mixing (done by moving the liquid in and out of the pipette several times), a fresh sterile pipette is used to transfer 1 cm^3 of the diluted sample into another tube containing 9 cm^3 of autoclaved water. This brings the dilution down to 1 in 100 or 1%.
3 The process is repeated twice more to produce dilutions of 1 in 1000 and 1 in 10 000 respectively.
4 Next, starting with the most dilute sample, a sterile pipette is used to withdraw 1 cm^3 of each of the dilutions for mixing with melted sterile nutrient agar to form what are known as **pour plates**.
5 All these manipulations should be done aseptically to avoid contamination. The plates are then incubated for 48 hours.

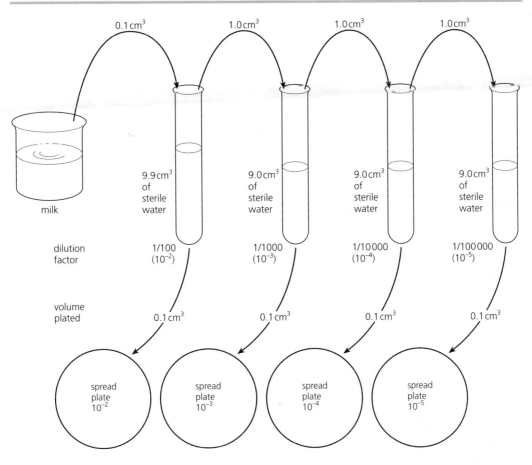

Calculations

Suppose that the total number of colonies on the 10^{-4} plate is 35

Number of viable colonies in $1\,cm^3$ of 10^{-4} dilution of milk

$= 35 \times 1/0.1$
$= 350$

Therefore, the number of viable bacteria in $1\,cm^3$ of the original milk sample

$= 350 \times 1/10^{-4}$
$= 350 \times 10^4$
$= 3.50 \times 10^6$

Figure 2.4 The dilution and plating method for estimating the number of bacteria in a sample of milk

Plates with between 30 and 300 colonies are chosen for counting. Less than 30 colonies is considered an unreliably small sample. More than 300 colonies is also considered unsatisfactory because the colonies may overlap and be mistakenly counted as single units. The results are expressed as **colony forming units (CFUs)** rather than numbers of bacteria, because it is never certain that each colony is formed from a single bacterium. From the number of colonies counted and the dilutions, the numbers of CFUs per cm^3 of the raw sample can be worked out.

The dilution and plating technique is the most reliable method of estimating the number of viable (living) bacteria in a sample. The main sources of error are low counts due to cells aggregating in clumps and the hot medium debilitating some types of heat-sensitive bacteria during the preparation of the pour plates.

Turbidimetry

This method is based on the observation that as a bacterial culture grows in a clear liquid, the culture becomes increasingly **turbid** (cloudy). The cloudiness is caused by the individual bacterial cells scattering light that strikes them. Since the bacterial cells are all roughly of the same size, the higher the density of the cells, the greater the amount of light scattered and the lesser the amount of light transmitted through the culture. A measure of the amount of light transmitted can therefore be used as an indirect measure of the bacterial cell concentration. A **spectrophotometer** is used to measure light transmission. '

The main advantage of this method is that it is quick and sensitive. Inaccuracies, however, can arise from the presence of debris and dead cells. The method is also not suitable for microorganisms that tend to settle in clumps at the bottom of the tube.

Growth curves

If the growth of a population of microorganisms is measured at regular intervals of time and the data are plotted on to a sheet of graph paper, a **sigmoid** or **S-shaped curve** is obtained (see Figure 2.5).

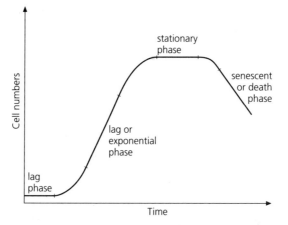

Figure 2.5 A sigmoid or S-shaped growth curve of a population of bacteria

The growth curve can be divided into four main phases. These are:

1 the **lag phase**
2 the **log** or **exponential growth phase**
3 the **stationary phase**
4 the **senescent** or **death phase**.

The lag phase

The lag phase is characterised by little or no increase in cell numbers, even though the cells may be metabolically active. It is a period of adjustment to new conditions. For example, additional ribosomes may need to be synthesised to permit a faster rate of enzyme production.

The log or exponential growth phase

This is a period of rapid growth during which the population increases by doubling and redoubling. Food is in plentiful supply and the conditions for growth are ideal. The microorganisms feed, grow and multiply at a rate that is as fast as their innate capacity or genetic constitution will allow. Two cells divide to become four, the four will increase to eight and so on. This is **exponential** or **logarithmic** growth.

After a period of exponential growth, the habitat becomes overcrowded with individuals each needing a supply of food. Competition for food leaves some cells with not enough for growth and reproduction. Toxic waste products may also accumulate to inhibitory levels. Fewer cells divide and the growth curve departs from its steeply rising path and starts to flatten out. During this period of transition to the stationary phase, the number of cells produced declines even though it remains higher than the number that are dying.

The stationary phase

Population growth falls to zero when the number of cells produced is exactly balanced by the number that are dying. When this stage is reached, the population is said to be in its **stationary phase**. To conserve energy, many cells stop multiplying. Some may even undergo changes associated with endospore formation. The lower metabolic activity of the cells makes them less susceptible to inhibition by metabolic poisons, such as antibiotics.

The senescent or death phase

Accumulation of toxic wastes or lack of food or oxygen may produce conditions that are unfavourable for maintaining life. When the death rate reaches exponential levels, the population is said to be in its **senescent** or **death phase**.

Calculations of growth rate constants

The sequence of numbers 1, 2, 4, 8, 16, 32, 64, 128, 256 etc., can be rewritten in exponential form as follows 2^0, 2^1, 2^2, 2^3, 2^4, 2^5, 2^6, 2^7, 2^8, etc. The advantage of writing numbers in this form becomes apparent when you come to multiplications and divisions of large numbers. For example, 16×32 becomes $2^4 \times 2^5 = 2^9$. Similarly, $256 \div 64$ becomes $2^8 \div 2^6 = 2^2$. Instead of multiplying numbers, you add exponents and instead of dividing numbers, you subtract exponents.

Suppose that to start with the number of bacteria in a culture is N_0. After one doubling, it would be $2^1 N_0$. After two doublings, it would be $2^2 N_0$ and after n doublings, the number of bacteria in the culture (N_n) would be $2^n N_0$.

An actual estimate of the numbers N_0 and N_n can be made with a Petroff–Hauser counting chamber or by the dilution-plating method. Having made these measurements, the next task is to work out the value of n, that is, the number of doublings that occurred between the start of the culture (N_0) to the time it became N_n. This can be done by taking logarithms as follows:

$$N_n = 2^n N_0$$

therefore, $$\log N_n = \log N_0 + n \log 2$$

therefore, $$n = \log N_n - \log N_0 \div \log 2$$

For example, if there were 18 000 bacteria in the culture to start with and after three hours the population had increased to 824 000, the number of generations, n, produced during that period of time would be:

$$n = (\log 824\ 000 - \log 18\ 000) \div \log 2$$
$$= (5.92 - 4.26) \div 0.30$$
$$= 5.53$$

From the time interval between the two measurements and the number of generations, n, one could work out the mean generation time, t, that is the time in minutes it takes for the population to double. In the example given above, it would be the time intervals between the two samples (180 minutes) divided by the number of generations (5.53), which works out to be 32.5 minutes.

For unicellular microorganisms that are multiplying by binary fission at a constant rate, the number of generations per hour, k, which is known as the exponential growth constant, can be worked out using the formula:

$$k = 60 \div t$$

where t is the mean generation time. In the example given above,

$$k = 60 \div 32.5$$
$$= 1.85$$

Diauxic growth

When two sources of carbon are available, some bacteria may preferentially metabolise one source until it is depleted before starting to metabolise the other. For example, when *E. coli* is cultured in a medium containing both glucose and lactose it will consume all the glucose first before switching to lactose. This biphasic response is known as **diauxie**. A diauxic growth curve for a population of bacteria shows a lag phase separating two exponential growth phases (Figure 2.6).

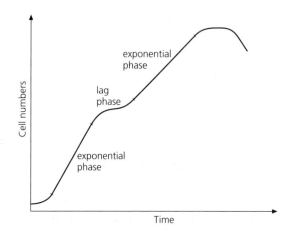

Figure 2.6 Diauxic growth curve of a population of bacteria

Glucose is a more readily utilisable source of carbon than lactose. To avoid losing out in competition for glucose to other microorganisms, *E. coli* has evolved a mechanism that normally keeps its genes for lactose metabolism repressed. It needs an absence of glucose and the presence of lactose for its genes for lactose metabolism to be switched on.

Examination questions

1 The diagram shows part of a haemocytometer grid viewed at a magnification of ×700. The triple-lined square measures 0.2 mm × 0.2 mm. The chamber contains a yeast suspension at a depth of 0.1 mm.

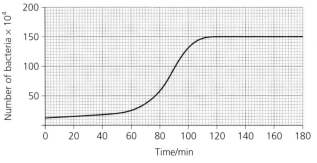

a Assuming that this triple-lined square is typical of all the squares on the haemocytometer grid, how many yeast cells are there in 1 mm³ of the solution? Show your working. (3)

b The dilution factor of the sample counted was ×10⁻³. How many yeast cells were there in 1 mm³ of the original suspension? (1)

(total = 4)

NEAB, June 1995

2 a The graph below shows the growth of a population of the bacterium *Escherichia coli* in liquid culture.

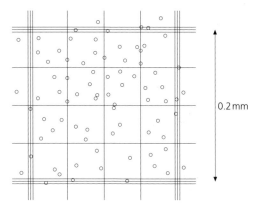

0.2 mm

i) What is the population size after 120 minutes? (1)

ii) Calculate the rate of growth of the population between 60 and 100 minutes. (3)

iii) The culture was provided with 1% glucose in the medium as the principal energy source. Explain the shape of the curve. (3)

b Further experiments may be carried out to investigate the effect of different sugars on the population growth.

i) Suggest **three** conditions which would have to be controlled. (3)

ii) List the steps needed to estimate the number of living bacteria in the population. (4)

(total = 14)

UODLE, June 1995

3 a i) Describe how you would prepare a 1×10^6 dilution of a bacterial culture. (4)

ii) To estimate the population density of the culture, several plates are inoculated with a number of different dilutions of the culture. Why is it usual to inoculate several plates with each separate dilution? (1)

b An agar plate inoculated with 0.1 cm^3 of a 1×10^6 dilution produced 31 colonies of bacteria. Calculate the population of bacteria that would be found in 1 cm^3 of the original culture. Show your working. (2)

(total = 7)

ULEAC, June 1996

Suggestions for learning experiences

Activity 7.3 Using the microscope to count cells (Skills and techniques) *Advanced Biology Study Guide*, CG Clegg and DG Mackean with PH Openshaw and RC Reynolds. John Murray (Publishers) Ltd 1996, page 98.

Activity 25.1 Basics of bacteriology (Skills and techniques/Investigation) *Advanced Biology Study Guide*, CG Clegg and DG Mackean with PH Openshaw and RC Reynolds. John Murray (Publishers) Ltd 1996, page 284.

Activity 25.2 Bacterial contamination of stale milk (Investigation) *Advanced Biology Study Guide*, CG Clegg and DG Mackean with PH Openshaw and RC Reynolds. John Murray (Publishers) Ltd 1996, page 287.

Work Card 3 Sorting microbes into groups *Practical Microbiology and Biotechnology for Schools*, Paul Wymer. Macdonald Educational 1987.

Biotechnology – an overview

Origins

Biotechnology is the science devoted to the harnessing and exploitation of biological processes, systems or organisms in manufacturing, agriculture and in the service industries. It is the youngest of the sciences but its roots go back 5000 years to the ancient Sumerians and Babylonians, who (without knowing it) used yeast to make a kind of beer. Instead of hops, which the Sumerians had no knowledge of, they flavoured their brew with cinnamon. Later, around 4000BC, the Egyptians discovered that the gas generated by brewer's yeast could leaven bread. Other fermentation processes with roots in antiquity include the use of *Acetobacter* bacteria to make vinegar, *Lactobacillus* bacteria to make yoghurt and various types of bacteria and moulds to make cheese.

One fermented food with a rural origin and a history that goes back thousands of years is **soy sauce**. It is a salty, brown liquid, which is widely used in Oriental cooking and which is commonly found on supermarket shelves. Its production requires two microbial transformations. A mould fungus, *Aspergillus oryzae*, converts the starch present in a salty broth of cooked soybeans and crushed wheat to fermentable sugars. The sugary mash is then allowed to ferment, for six months to a year or more, in the presence of lactic acid bacteria and yeast. The resulting liquid is soy sauce.

Milestones in the development of biotechnology

Seventeenth century – Antony van Leeuwenhoek discovers microorganisms

The ancient art of preparing food and drink by fermentation continued until the seventeenth century without the existence of microorganisms being recognised. Then Antony van Leeuwenhoek (1632–1723), a Dutch textile merchant, described seeing 'tiny animalcules prettily a moving' in a drop of pond water and in scrapings from between his teeth. Leeuwenhoek's descriptions of bacteria were accurate enough for today's microbiologists to recognise the species of bacteria he was describing.

Figure 3.1 Antony van Leeuwenhoek (1632–1723)

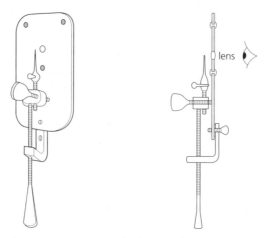

Figure 3.2 Drawings of Antony van Leeuwenhoek's simple microscope

Leeuwenhoek spent much of his spare time grinding lenses. Some of his lenses were no bigger than tomato seeds. He made hundreds of tiny lenses which he mounted between two thin sheets of silver or brass. The edges of the lenses were covered by the metal plates leaving a small central area exposed. Through these simple microscopes Leeuwenhoek could see objects magnified 40–275 times. He used his lenses to look at all kinds of objects including a drop of water from a pond and scrapings from between his teeth. The object to be viewed was placed at the tip of a needle whose height and distance from the lens could be adjusted by means of screws. Using his simple microscopes, Leeuwenhoek described seeing what we now know as bacteria.

1861 – Louis Pasteur proves that fermentative processes are caused by microorganisms

Louis Pasteur (1822–1895) lived at a time when it was widely believed that microorganisms arose spontaneously from non-living matter. To the people of his day, it seemed to explain why clear broth became, after a period of time, clouded with large numbers of microbes. By means of a series of elegant experiments, Pasteur convincingly put the theory of spontaneous generation to rest. Later, Pasteur showed that each type of fermentation was caused by a specific type of microorganism.

Figure 3.3 Louis Pasteur (1822–1895)

In 1861, Pasteur, performed the landmark 'swan-neck' flasks experiment that demolished the theory of spontaneous generation. Pasteur had been working with microbes. He reasoned in the following way. Since microbes are very small and light, they must be present on Earth nearly everywhere. Some must be present floating in the air. But microbes are most probably denser than air and, like dust particles, should eventually settle.

Figure 3.4 Louis Pasteur in his laboratory

In his experiment, Pasteur poured nutrient broth into a number of flasks and then drew the necks of the flasks out into long tubes, which he bent into S-shaped curves. He boiled the broths in the flasks to kill any microorganisms present in them. The vapour from the boiling broth forced out the air from within the flasks but air slowly returned when the flasks were left to cool. Pasteur reasoned, however, that any microbes that were present floating in the air, being heavier, would settle in the moisture that condensed on the sides of the long S-shaped necks of the flasks. In this way, the air entering the flasks would be washed free of dust and microbes. The boiled broth should therefore remain clear and sterile.

Sure enough, when months later Pasteur opened the flasks, the broth within them was found to be clear, sweet smelling and unchanged. However, if he cut off the neck of a flask or tipped a little of the nutrient broth into the neck and allowed the contaminated liquid to run back into the flask, within 24 to 48 hours, the broth would turn cloudy and start to smell bad.

Pasteur's experiment with 'swan-neck' flasks provided convincing answers to two objections by believers of spontaneous generation. Firstly, he proved that heat did not chemically alter the broth and, secondly, that even if fresh air was available the broth did not spontaneously putrefy. He suggested that food left standing around went bad because microbes were carried to it through the air.

1866 – Gregor Mendel, experimenting with pea plants, describes the mechanism of inheritance

Gregor Mendel (1822–1884) was an Austrian monk who worked on pea plants that he cultivated with great care in his garden. By studying one trait at a time, for example vine height or seed colour, he simplified his study of inheritance and worked out the laws that govern how characteristics are passed from parents to offspring. In 1866, after eight years of patient work, Mendel published his findings. His work was, however, so far ahead of its time that no one understood the significance of his discoveries. In 1900, 16 years after his death, Mendel's pioneering work on inheritance was independently rediscovered by three workers in three different countries and recognised for its greatness.

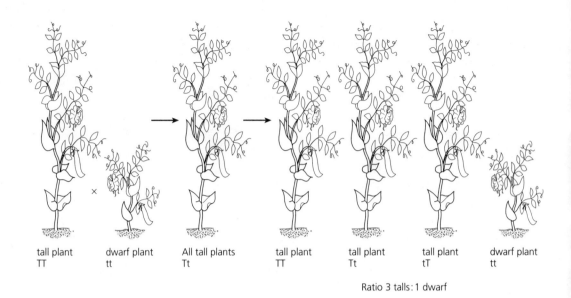

| tall plant | dwarf plant | All tall plants | tall plant | tall plant | tall plant | dwarf plant |
| TT | tt | Tt | TT | Tt | tT | tt |

Ratio 3 talls : 1 dwarf

Figure 3.5 Drawings illustrating one of Mendel's crosses involving pea plants

Gregor Mendel carried out a number of experiments on the pea plant. He noticed that some pea plants were tall, some short. Some had pods that looked fully blown up, others had shrunken pods. Some had pea cases that were yellow, others green. In all, Mendel studied seven traits that could be readily distinguished and identified.

In one experiment, Mendel pollinated tall pea plants with the pollen obtained from dwarf plants and vice versa. He waited for the fertilised ovules to mature into seeds and then gathered and sowed the seeds. The seedlings that emerged all grew into tall plants. None were dwarf. When these hybrid offspring (known as **F₁** or **first filial generation**) produced flowers, Mendel allowed them to self-pollinate (which was the normal habit of garden pea plants). The following year Mendel sowed the seeds and obtained plants that were second generation offspring (F_2). Out of 1064 F_2 plants, 787 were tall and 277 were dwarf. The trait for dwarfness, missing from the F_1 plants, had reappeared in the F_2.

Mendel reasoned that the factor for dwarfness must have been present in some latent form in the F_1 hybrids. Since the factor for dwarfness was hidden by the factor for tallness, he called the tallness factor **dominant** and the factor that receded he called **recessive**. Mendel then went on to explain his F_2 results and this was where he showed his real genius. From what appeared to be useless bits of information, he came up with a simple explanation that knitted together all the facts. He noticed that 787 tall plants to 277 dwarf plants gave a ratio of 2.81 : 1. In similar crosses with pea plants, involving other contrasting characteristics, again only the dominant trait showed up in the F_1, whereas in the F_2, he obtained a mixed population with plants showing the dominant trait outnumbering those with the recessive trait by a ratio of 3 : 1.

Although chromosomes had not yet been discovered, Mendel concluded that the factors determining the characteristics of individuals must have been passed from parents to offspring through the pollen grains and egg cells. He hypothesised that every individual has two factors (now called genes) for each trait – one derived from the male parent and the other from the female parent. He then went on to assign a capital letter to symbolise a dominant factor and a small letter for a recessive factor. In a cross between tall and dwarf pea plants, the true-breeding tall plant (one that always reproduces tall plants from generation to generation) would have the genetic constitution (or genotype) TT. The true-breeding dwarf plant would have the genetic constitution tt. Mendel went on to explain that when he affected his artificial cross between the tall and the dwarf plants, the tall parent contributed a single T and the dwarf parent a single t, thus producing hybrid offspring with a genotype Tt (the term 'genotype' was introduced later as a modern refinement). Since T is dominant over t, the F_1 hybrids were all tall.

Mendel postulated that the F_1 hybrids were each capable of producing two types of male and two types of female gametes. Half the male gametes would carry the dominant factor, T, and the other half would carry the recessive factor, t. The same would be true of the female gametes. By the laws of chance, a male gamete carrying T would have equal probability of combining with a female gamete carrying either T or t. The same would be true of the male gametes carrying t. The random combination of these two types of male and female gametes would result in equal numbers of four types of zygotes, namely TT, Tt, tT and tt. Pea plants with TT would be tall. So would pea plants with Tt or tT, as T is dominant. Those with tt would be dwarf. Thus, three-quarters of the F_2 offspring would be tall and one-quarter would be dwarf, giving a ratio of 3 talls : 1 dwarf.

Mendel put forward the following general rule with regard to genetic inheritance. Known as the **Law of segregation** it states that within every individual, a pair of factors (or genes) controls each trait and that during gamete formation, the factors, acting like particles, separate so that each gamete receives only one member of each pair.

1896 – Eduard Buchner discovers that fermentations are brought about by non-living chemicals (enzymes) produced by living cells

Eduard Buchner (1860–1917), a German chemist, won the Nobel Prize for Chemistry in 1907 for demonstrating that it was not the living cells themselves but certain 'vital substances' that were responsible for the fermentation of carbohydrates. In 1896, he ground yeast cells with sand until no more intact cells were left. He then filtered the liquid to remove the sand and quite by accident added sugar to the filtrate. To his surprise, he found that the non-living extract of yeast cells retained the ability of converting sugar to alcohol and carbon dioxide. Later, his vital factors turned out to be a class of very useful proteins called **enzymes**.

1928 – Alexander Fleming discovers penicillin

In 1928, Alexander Fleming (1881–1955) was examining culture plates containing *Staphylococcus aureus*, a bacterium that causes skin infections such as boils, when he noticed a green mould growing in one of the Petri dishes. Since he was trying to grow a pure culture of the staphylococcus, such a contaminated dish would normally have been thrown away. Fleming, however, looked closely at the dish and he noticed that there was a clear area around the mould where no bacteria were growing. It gave him the idea that the green mould, *Penicillium notatum*, was producing something that was 'dissolving' the bacteria around it. Fleming made a photograph of the culture plate (see Figure 3.7).

Figure 3.6 Sir Alexander Fleming (1881–1955) working in his laboratory

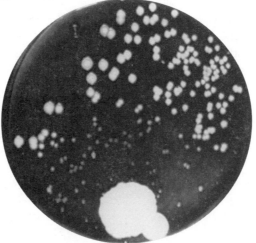

Figure 3.7 Photograph of Alexander Fleming's original culture plate showing a colony of *Penicillium* inhibiting the growth of staphylococci (white dots)

He then transferred a few spores of the mould on to agar in Petri dishes and began to culture more of the mould. Later, he succeeded in growing the mould in nutrient broth. From the broth he obtained a filtrate that was capable of inhibiting the growth of many types of bacteria. Fleming injected large doses of the broth filtrate into rabbits and white mice and showed that it was non-toxic to animals. He named the active substance in the filtrate **penicillin**. He tried to extract penicillin as a pure chemical but its instability frustrated his efforts. After trying for four years, Fleming abandoned the work in 1932.

1940s – Sterile techniques and complicated engineering are applied to the mass cultivation of microorganisms in the manufacture of antibiotics and other industrial chemicals

In 1939 two British scientists, Professor Howard Florey and Dr Ernst Chain, successfully prepared a stable form of penicillin which was shown to be remarkably effective against bacterial diseases in experimental animals. In 1941, Britain was at war and Florey went to the United States to interest the US Department of Agriculture and several American pharmaceutical companies in manufacturing penicillin. A related mould *Penicillium chrysogenum*, which was found growing on melons in the local market, was eventually chosen for mass cultivation because it proved to be a better producer of penicillin than *P. notatum*. Not long after that, mass production of penicillin became a reality and thousands of war-wounded soldiers were saved from dying of gangrene and other bacterial infections.

The successful manufacture of penicillin was a major landmark event because several technological problems were overcome by a system of complicated engineering. Sterile techniques were also applied to the mass culture of a selected microorganism on an industrial scale for the first time. (See Chapter 4, page 58.)

1953 – James Watson and Francis Crick discover the double-helical structure of DNA

In 1950 James Watson, a biochemist, came out of a Danish Royal Society lecture in Copenhagen feeling quite inspired after he had listened to a novel approach in the study of proteins by the building of three-dimensional, scale models of proteins. Back in Cambridge a year later, Watson met Francis Crick, a PhD physics student and they decided to collaborate. They built scale models of the component parts of the DNA molecule and then attempted to fit the parts together to form a three-dimensional model that would conform with all the known facts about DNA. In

Figure 3.8 James Watson and Francis Crick exhibit their double-helical model of DNA in 1953

April 1953, they published their 'double-helical' structure of DNA, which quickly gained wide acceptance. Their discovery led to the flowering of a new branch of biology known as **molecular biology**.

1972 – Paul Berg and others at Stanford University combine the DNA of two viruses in a test tube to produce the first recombinant DNA molecules

Paul Berg, who is often described as 'the father of genetic engineering', was studying cell differentiation and the way in which gene expression is controlled. It occurred to him that if he could remove specific genes from the chromosome of one organism and somehow splice these genes on to the chromosome of an unrelated organism, he would have an ideal way of studying gene expression. By a procedure involving several steps, each catalysed by a different enzyme, Berg succeeded in constructing the first recombinant DNA molecules from the DNA of two different types of viruses. An outline of his procedure is illustrated in Figure 3.9.

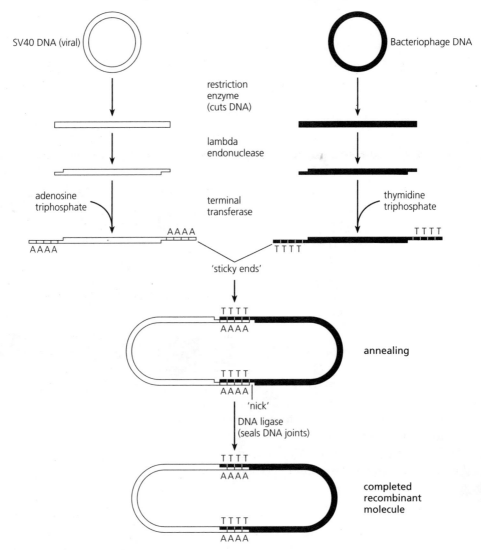

Figure 3.9 A summary of the procedure that Paul Berg used to construct the first recombinant molecule

1973 – Stanley Cohen and Herbert Boyer succeed in inserting recombinant DNA into host bacteria that then reproduce (or clone) the foreign DNA

Stanley Cohen (Stanford University) and Herbert Boyer (University of California) invented the technique for transplanting functional genes extracted from different organisms into bacteria. They succeeded in splicing together two different **plasmids** (small circular pieces of DNA found in bacteria) and then introducing the recombinant DNA molecules into living *Escherichia coli*. The genetically altered bacteria then replicated, expressing the information carried by the alien genes. They had, in other words, created the first genetically engineered bacteria. Their accomplishment marked the start of a new kind of industrial revolution based on genetic engineering. (Details of how genetic engineering is accomplished are described in Chapter 5.)

1980 – A United States Supreme Court rules that 'a live human-made microorganism is patentable matter'

This was an important ruling because it led to the establishment of a number of highly successful biotechnology companies in the US and in other parts of the world. Patents are open letters that protect an inventor from imitation. Without the protection of patents few companies, especially pharmaceutical ones, would be prepared to invest in expensive research if their innovations could be copied by rival companies. Pharmaceutical companies estimate that it costs GB£25 million to convert a laboratory stage idea into a marketable drug. Had the Supreme Court ruling gone the other way, biotechnology companies might have been tempted to protect their business through secrecy, thus slowing down progress through the free exchange of ideas.

1982 – Human insulin produced by genetically engineered bacteria is marketed under the trade name Humulin

The marketing of human insulin produced the first commercial fruits for recombinant DNA technology. Insulin, traditionally extracted in limited quantities from pigs and cattle, was now being produced cheaply and in unlimited quantities by culturing bacteria that were given the human gene for insulin. Millions of diabetics throughout the world benefited from this new technology. (Details of the manufacture of human insulin are described in Chapter 5.)

1994 – The world's first genetically modified food (a tomato designed to be tastier) receives approval for release into the high-street shops in California

After years of scrutiny, the US Food and Drug Administration cleared the way for the sale of tomatoes genetically engineered to contain an antisense gene that slows down the natural softening process as the fruit ripens (see Chapter 5 for details). This increases the shelf-lives of the fruits; it also allows the fruits to be left to ripen on the vine before being picked for transport to the shops. The British Environment Secretary gave clearance for the sale of these genetically engineered, tastier tomatoes in Britain in 1996.

Today, 1997

We are today in the middle of a biotechnological revolution. It is a new type of industrial and agricultural revolution based not on coal and steel but on the exploitation of microorganisms and the development of high-performance genetically modified crop plants. The factories that constitute the new industrial revolution consist of billions of microorganisms cultured in huge, stainless steel vats that emit no smoke or environmental pollutants. The products include healthier foods, purer pharmaceuticals, 'greener' industrial materials and renewable, environmentally friendly fuels, for example bioethanol.

Biotechnology today extends its umbrella over all kinds of industrial processes, such as the manufacture of cheese, beer and industrial enzymes, the production of vaccines and medicine, the treatment of sewage and the development of genetically engineered crop plants. The impact of biotechnology can be seen in the biological washing powders we use, the biscuits we eat, the medicines that we take and the diagnostic kits (like pregnancy tests) that are available over the counter at the local chemist. Biotechnological companies today constitute a multi-billion pound industry and are strongly featured in the stock markets of the world. They are at the forefront of industrial development and are likely to feature even more strongly in the future.

In agriculture, the list of crop plants that have been genetically engineered to be resistant to insect pests and pathogenic fungi is rapidly growing longer. Bananas that have been genetically engineered to produce vaccines, as a cheap way of protecting children from life-threatening diseases, are already a reality. Fish farms have recently been started in Scotland for growing genetically engineered salmon; these fish have growth rates 10 times faster than ordinary salmon. By saving on pond maintenance and losses through disease, the fish farmers are hoping to boost their profits.

Figure 3.10 Natural Pacific salmon (left) and genetically altered Pacific salmon (right)

Prospects for the future

Further 'miraculous' discoveries will undoubtedly be made both in pure biological research and in biotechnology. Humankind will continue to reap further benefits from the exploitation of nature's own biochemical tools. The links between industry and academic research in the universities will probably strengthen, with industries funding a greater share of pure research especially in the field of molecular biology. New medicines that target viruses and cancer without harming healthy tissues are a distinct prospect in the not too distant future. We can certainly look forward to the arrival of 'perfect' vaccines that are both effective and safe. Thanks to biotechnology, people can also expect to be able to assess their risk of impending disease and possibly even take early steps to correct genetic disorders.

In the field of agriculture and food production, advances in biotechnology will undoubtedly continue to ease the pressure on food supplies resulting from an expanding human population. Many more crop plants will be genetically engineered to be disease-resistant and to produce bumper harvests. There is also the likely possibility that the genetic breakthrough would be made to allow subtropical crops, like sugar cane and millet, to grow in temperate climates such as in France or southern England.

Grain crops such as maize and wheat may successfully be genetically altered to fix their own atmospheric nitrogen and thus become less dependent on chemical fertilisers (see Chapter 6, page 87). Another major prize would be the development of genetically engineered fruits or vegetables that would not only be tastier and more nutritious, but which would also function as in-field fermenters for the production of antibodies against life-threatening diseases such as AIDS.

Biotechnology can also be expected to play an increased role in underpinning humankind's efforts at pollution control. Research into anaerobic digestion may lead to improvements in plant design and more effective ways of dealing with municipal rubbish. Photosynthetic microorganisms, such as *Chlorella*, may assume greater importance as a source of renewable energy fuel. A way may be found to cultivate them in sunny parts of the world to provide biomass for use as a fuel for generating electricity at an economic price. It may even one day be possible to ferment wood and convert it into 'liquid gold' – bioethanol.

Questions

1 What is biotechnology?
2 Give three ways by which the biotechnology of today differs from the 'biotechnology' of ancient times.

Suggestions for learning experiences

Work Card 2 Pasteur's experiment *Practical Microbiology and Biotechnology for Schools* by Paul Wymer. Macdonald Educational, 1987.

4 Fermenter technology

Strictly speaking, **fermentation** is the partial breakdown of organic substrates by microorganisms under anaerobic conditions. The fermentation of sugar to alcohol by yeast is a well-known example. Over the years, however, biotechnologists have used the term 'fermentation' to refer to any large-scale culture of microorganisms under aerobic or anaerobic conditions. A **fermenter** is any vessel that is used for the bulk culture of microorganisms or even plant cells, regardless of whether or not any actual fermentation in the strict sense of the term is occurring within it. A preferred term is a **bioreactor** because it reflects more accurately the function of the vessel.

The 'technology' in fermentation technology refers to the complicated engineering needed to provide and maintain optimum conditions for the culture of the chosen microorganisms and also for the handling of the reaction products. It usually manifests itself as batteries of gleaming, stainless steel bioreactors, their auxiliary vessels and what appears to the untrained eye as a complicated system of pipes, pumps and valves. There are also monitoring devices, usually linked to an array of computers, that automatically work the pumps and stirrers, and open and shut the valves.

The bioreactor

A vat or reaction vessel known as a **bioreactor** together with its system of pipes, pumps, valves, probes and other devices is generally used to create the optimum physical and chemical conditions within a protected environment for the microorganisms to grow and function efficiently. Most industrial bioreactors are huge (capacities of about 200 m^3 are common); they are usually made of stainless steel. Not only are they able to withstand the high internal pressures caused by gases produced during the catalytic reactions taking place within the bioreactor, the stainless steel vessels are also non-corrosive and can be made to have hard, smooth internal surfaces that can be thoroughly washed and disinfected before use.

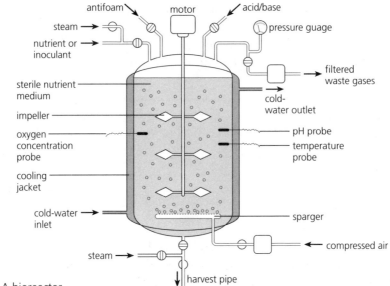

Figure 4.1 A bioreactor

Advantages of using biological processes

- Enzymatic reactions occur at low temperatures whereas non-biological reactions generally demand a high input of energy to heat up or cool down the reaction vessel.
- Enzymes are specific. They usually catalyse just one kind of reaction. Inorganic catalysts are less specific. They tend, therefore, to yield unwanted by-products, which may have to be removed in a separate purification procedure.
- Biological processes use water as a solvent. Non-biological processes generally require the use of more expensive chemical solvents.
- Enzymes are biodegradable substances; inorganic catalysts are generally non-biodegradable and may contribute to environmental pollution.

Sterilisation and aseptic entry

Most industrial fermentation processes make use of just one strain of microorganism. Procedures must therefore be set in place to prevent contamination by unwanted microorganisms. The bioreactor, its pipes, valves and other devices that come in contact with the nutrient medium must be sterilised by the use of steam for 30 to 60 minutes. All incoming nutrients must also be sterilised by steam treatment (or, in some cases, by filtration). The incoming air must also be filtered to exclude airborne microorganisms. The integrity of the exit points should also be maintained by appropriate aseptic techniques.

Contamination by unwanted microorganisms could disrupt a biotechnological process in a number of ways:

1 the unwanted microorganisms could inhibit or destroy the enzyme or the culture of living cells
2 they could destroy the reaction products
3 they could contaminate the reaction products with their toxic waste.

Maintaining optimum conditions

Biological systems are very sensitive to changes in temperature and pH. As a result, most bioreactors are equipped with devices that continually monitor and automatically adjust the temperature and pH within the reactor. Auxiliary tanks are generally provided for the addition of acid or alkali, nutrients and antifoam. Refrigerated water is usually circulated through a jacket surrounding the tank to remove heat produced by microbial activity.

Many bioreactors have built-in mechanical stirrers, which mix the contents of the watery medium. Good mixing is needed to:

- distribute the nutrients and the population of microorganisms evenly
- ensure rapid distribution of additives and control of pH
- promote even distribution of heat and oxygen (if the process is aerobic) and thus help to maintain uniform conditions throughout the culture medium.

49

Scale-up

Scale-up is the process of taking a small-scale laboratory production to a large-scale process of economic value. The aim in scale-up is to maintain optimal operating conditions during the change-over from a small-scale laboratory research project to a large-scale commercial installation. The scale-up process is not as straightforward as it may at first appear. The difficulty is that a small quantity of microorganisms in a laboratory-sized research vessel seldom behave in the same way as a tonne of the same microorganisms in a pilot plant.

If the microorganisms are aerobic they can, when present in huge numbers, rapidly consume the dissolved oxygen supply. Pure oxygen may therefore need to be pumped in; this can be expensive. To persuade more oxygen to dissolve, the size of the air bubbles may need to be reduced and the rate of oxygen supply may need to be increased. Sparging smaller air bubbles through a liquid medium, however, requires a greater input of energy, which can add to the cost of production. The smaller bubbles could also interfere with the growth of the microorganisms and could create foaming problems, which would need to be controlled with antifoam (another expense). The rate of stirring and the concentration of nutrients may therefore need to be adjusted during scale-up. The physical presence of a large body of microorganisms can create viscosity problems, which can put the impellers under mechanical stress.

Some types of filamentous fungi settle on the inside surface of the reaction vessel, making stirring less effective; others may settle on the probes or grow within the inlet and exit pipes, causing them to become blocked; others may aggregate in clumps, making it difficult to supply enough oxygen to those microorganisms growing at the centre of the growing clumps.

An increase in size comes with implications regarding heat production and losses. Consider a small cube of dimensions 1 cm – its surface area is 6 cm^2 and its volume is 1 cm^3, giving it a surface area to volume ratio of 6 : 1 = 6 (Figure 4.2). Now consider a larger cube with dimensions of 10 cm – its surface area is 600 cm^2 and its volume is 1000 cm^3, giving it a surface area to volume ratio of 600 : 1000 = 0.6. In other words, an increase in geometric size means a faster rate of increase in mass or volume as compared with surface area. Or, to put it in another way, surface area increases as the square of the linear dimensions, whereas volume or mass increases as the cube of the linear dimensions. Since heat production is proportional to mass or volume, and heat losses, which occur through the surface, are proportional to surface area, it follows that scale-up has its problems regarding how to stop the fermenter from overheating due to microbial cell respiration.

Refrigerated water, circulated through a jacket fitted to the outside of the bioreactor, is normally used to cool the fermenter. Where jackets do not offer sufficient surface area for heat transfer, coiled tubes installed inside the bioreactor may provide additional surface area for heat transfer. However, unless the coils can be thoroughly cleaned between batches, they can pose a hygiene problem.

Of course, there is the sheer engineering task of handling, containing, sterilising and incubating a huge volume of liquid, and then harvesting and extracting the desirable reaction products. There is also the capital cost of the equipment needed

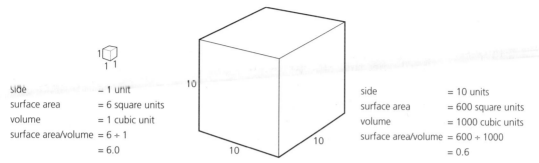

Figure 4.2 The larger the body, the smaller its surface area : volume ratio

for scale-up, operating costs (in terms of labour and raw materials) and the research and development costs, which must be taken into consideration and weighed against the value of the product.

In general, scale-up is done in a series of steps. A tenfold increase in size is the norm for each step. Mathematical models are usually available but adjustments are usually made by trial and error based on the process engineer's experience.

Scale-up at the school level

At the school level, the largest fermenters that can be purchased from recognised scientific suppliers (e.g. Scientific and Chemical Supplies Ltd, Bilston, West Midlands) for a scale-up investigation is a plastic fermenter of 5 litre capacity. Because such a vessel would be too large to fit into a standard-sized autoclave and also because of its plastic construction, the recommended method of sterilisation is by immersion in a standard sterilising chemical, such as Milton. The culture medium is sterilised separately in an autoclave or pressure cooker. Contamination by airborne microorganisms is a distinct possibility when the fermenter is opened to pour the sterile culture medium into the fermenter. The medium is maintained at its incubation temperature via a thermostatically controlled aquarium heater. Electrical safety of the equipment is a factor that needs to be taken into consideration. The use of an RCD (residual current device) adaptor as a circuit-breaker is strongly recommended. Finally, there is the problem of disposal of the culture at the end of the investigation. The most convenient method is down the toilet, but this can be unacceptable if the culture is contaminated. Aerosol formation during this type of disposal is another major hazard.

Downstream processing

Downstream processing is the general term used to refer to the harvesting, extraction and preparation of the useful products for marketing at the completion of the fermentation phase of the process. For an industrial process involving large-scale culture of microorganisms, downstream processing usually involves:

- **separation** of the product from the microorganisms by filtration, centrifugation or flocculation (adding a chemical to cause the microorganisms to clump and settle to the bottom)

- **concentration** of the product by reverse osmosis, ultrafiltration or vacuum evaporation, etc.
- **purification** of the product by chromatography, affinity methods (e.g. using monoclonal antibodies that bind to the product, see purification of proteins, Chapter 8, page 00) or specific precipitation
- **packaging** the product for sale to consumers.

Questions

1 Describe two common problems associated with scale-up.
2 What is meant by 'downstream processing'?

Fermenter systems

There are two main fermenter systems for the large-scale culture of microorganisms:

1 a **batch (or closed) process**
2 a **continuous (or open) process**.

Batch processes

In the batch process, the vat or bioreactor is filled with the sterile nutrient medium. The chosen microorganisms are mixed in and allowed to grow until no more products are made. The vat is then emptied, the products harvested and the bioreactor is cleaned out, sterilised and made ready for its next run. Cheese, yoghurt, beer, bread and antibiotics are manufactured by batch processes.

Continuous processes

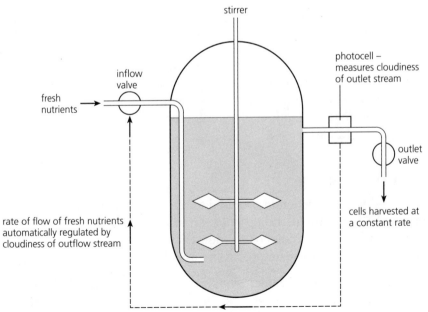

Figure 4.3 Continuous culture

In the continuous process, fresh sterile nutrient medium is continually fed into the fermenter and an equivalent amount of culture medium together with the reaction products is continually withdrawn. The rate of input is generally slightly less than the maximum rate of consumption of the nutrients. The production of single-cell proteins (SCPs) and mycoproteins are examples of continuous processes.

The two types of fermenter systems compared

	Batch process	Continuous process
Advantages	• Relatively easy to keep under control • Element of flexibility – bioreactors can be switched to the production of some other product to meet demand	• Process can be automated and production, once established, can go on day and night • Product volume is generally higher than a batch process of equivalent size
Disadvantages	• Element of tediousness – after each run it is necessary to start all over again (cleaning, sterilising, getting everything ready etc.) • The catalyst is generally discarded at the end of each batch. This can be costly, the cost being the equivalent to the cost for the nutrients consumed by the growing cells	• More vulnerable to contamination by unwanted microorganisms

Examples of fermenter systems
Manufacture of cheese

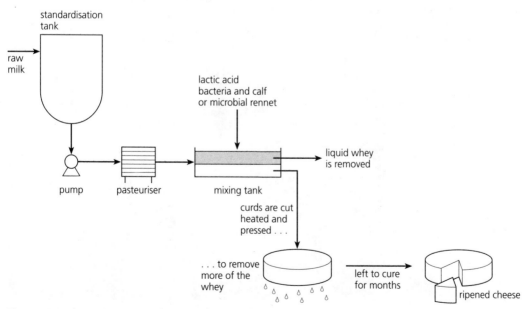

Figure 4.4 The main steps in the manufacture of cheese

Cheese is a product of the fermentation of milk. In the modern cheese-making process, the milk is first pasteurised to kill off any vegetative microorganisms. One or more selected strains of **lactic acid bacteria** (e.g. *Streptococcus lactis* or *Lactobacillus acidophilus*) are then stirred into the warm milk. The bacteria feed on the milk sugar lactose and anaerobically degrade it to **lactic acid**. The acid coagulates the milk proteins, causing the milk to separate into a solid part (known as **curd**) and a watery liquid part (known as **whey**). **Rennet**, traditionally extracted from the stomach of unweaned calves but more recently produced by genetically engineered bacteria, is added to the souring milk. Rennet contains the enzyme **chymosin** or **rennin**, which coagulates milk proteins.

The solid curds are then cut, heated and stirred to allow any whey trapped within the curds to be released. When the stirring stops, the curds settle to the bottom allowing the whey to be drained off. Salt is then added to act as a preservative and as a flavour enhancer. The curds are then poured into moulds, pressed to squeeze out more of the whey, wrapped in cloth and then left to ripen. During the ripening process, microbes growing in or on the rounds of cheese break down milk proteins into peptides rich in amino acids that enhance savoury tastes. Some fats are also broken down to fatty acids. Volatile thioesters may also be released, giving the cheese its characteristic aroma.

Yoghurt production

Figure 4.5 The production of yoghurt

Yoghurt is a semi-liquid product of fermented milk. A symbiotic mixture of two types of bacteria *Lactobacillus acidophilus* and *Streptococcus thermophilus*, in approximately equal proportions, is used to make yoghurt. The milk is heated to 85–95 °C for 15–30 minutes to drive out dissolved air and to denature the milk proteins. The milk is then cooled to the incubation temperature of 40–45 °C before the starter culture is stirred in. *L. acidophilus* makes the yoghurt by anaerobically degrading lactose to lactic acid. The acid coagulates milk proteins, thus thickening the yoghurt. *S. thermophilus* produces methanoic acid (formerly known as formic acid) and carbon dioxide, which together act as growth stimulants for *L. acidophilus*. In its turn, *L. acidophilus* releases peptides from the breakdown of milk proteins, which stimulate the growth of *S. thermophilus*. The characteristic flavour of natural yoghurt comes from the lactic acid and from ethanal (formerly known as acetaldehyde), a metabolic by-product released by both species of bacteria.

Many supermarket yoghurts are pasteurised before or after packaging to increase their shelf-life. Fruit pulp or fruit essences are also often added to make the product more appealing.

Manufacture of beer

Most beers are made from barley and hops. The process of beer brewing is divisible into seven stages known as **malting, kilning, milling, mashing, boiling, fermentation** and **finishing**.

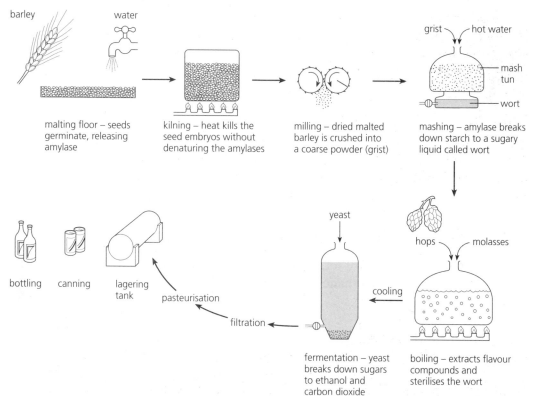

Figure 4.6 The commercial production of beer

Malting

Malting is the process during which barley seeds are steeped in water for one or two days and then spread over a warm, damp place and left for a further two to six days to allow the seeds to germinate. Gibberellic acid is sprayed on to the soaked seeds to speed up germination. During germination, amylases are mobilised by the developing embryos for hydrolysing the starch stored within the seeds to fermentable sugars (mainly maltose).

Kilning

The malt is then slowly dried by gradually heating to between 65 and 80 °C. This process, known as kilning, kills the embryos without destroying the amylases. The higher the kilning temperature, the darker the beer produced.

Milling

The dried barley grains are then crushed to a coarse powder known as **grist**.

Mashing

The grist is steeped in warm water and the resulting porridge-like **mash** is maintained at 65 °C for an hour to allow the amylases to break down the starch to fermentable sugars. Some starch remains undigested or only partly degraded to dextrins. Some brewers add amylases extracted from other sources to speed up the conversion of starch to sugars in order to get a low-carbohydrate or 'lite' beer. Mashing also allows the sugars, amino acids and mineral salts to diffuse out of the seeds into the aqueous liquid. (These nutrients are needed for growth of the yeast cells, which will be added later). The nutrient-rich liquor (called **sweet wort**) is then separated from the spent grains by filtration, leaving a residue that is gathered for use as cattle feed.

Boiling

Sugar, in the form of molasses, may be added to the sweet wort. It is then boiled with hops – a flower that gives beer its characteristic bitter taste. Boiling extracts the flavour compounds, stops further enzyme action and precipitates out tannins, proteins and phosphates that would otherwise make the beer cloudy.

Fermentation

The boiled wort is cooled to 30 °C and then inoculated with a selected strain of yeast. It is then left to ferment for 7–10 days. During fermentation the yeast degrades the sugars anaerobically to ethanol and carbon dioxide.

Finishing

When fermentation is completed, manufacturers filter the beer to remove the yeast and other impurities. A viscous solution called **isinglass** (made from the swim bladders of tropical fish) is added to flocculate the yeast into clumps to facilitate filtration. The brewer may then recycle the yeast or use it elsewhere to make food products (e.g. yeast extract). Traditional beers are stored in barrels and are allowed to 'condition'. Modern beers are pasteurised, standardised for colour and flavour and, finally, bottled or canned.

The final alcohol content of most beers is 3.5–5.0%. Most beers contain undigested starch residues, which are responsible for the characteristic 'beer belly' of habitual beer drinkers.

Manufacture of bread

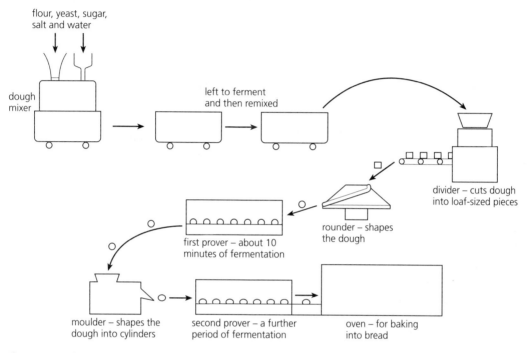

Figure 4.7 The main steps in the manufacture of bread

Bread is made by mixing wheat flour with water and smaller proportions of yeast, sugar, salt, vegetable fat, emulsifier and vitamin C. The ingredients are weighed and mixed. There are two crucial reactions during the **mixing** or **kneading** of the dough: the hydration of the **gluten** (the collective name for the proteins in the flour) and the poorly understood physical and chemical changes to the proteins, which coalesce into gluten fibrils and give the dough its silky, elastic and resilient texture. Doughs made from cereal flour other than wheat (e.g. rye or barley) contain less gluten, are less sticky and elastic, and are less capable of holding on to the leavening gases produced during the baking process. After mixing, the dough is **allowed to ferment** at 27 °C in a humid atmosphere. During this stage, the yeast, a strain of *Saccharomyces cerevisiae*, feeds on the sugar breaking it down anaerobically to ethanol and carbon dioxide. The bubbles of carbon dioxide remain trapped within the sticky dough causing it to rise. The dough then goes to what is known as the **make-up stage**, where it passes through a series of machines that cut the dough into loaf-sized pieces, mould them into shape and deposit them in baking pans. The dough then goes through a **final fermentation** or **proofing** stage at a temperature of 40 °C for 45 minutes before being put in the oven and **baked** for 25–40 minutes at 235 °C. The heat of the oven kills the yeast, evaporates the ethanol and cooks the flour. After baking, the loaves of bread are cooled, sliced and wrapped. A modern bakery can make about 10 000 loaves of bread per hour.

Questions

3 Name the two types of bacteria that are involved in yoghurt production and state their respective roles.

4 Explain the roles of:

   a sugar   **b** yeast   **c** water

   in the bread-making process.

5 Describe the main stages in the manufacture of beer.

Production of antibiotics

Antibiotics are organic compounds of low molecular weight produced by certain microorganisms that can kill or inhibit the growth of other microorganisms. They are examples of what are known as **secondary metabolites**. Unlike primary metabolites, like glucose, which are essential for cell survival, secondary metabolites are not essential for the day-to-day survival of the organism that produces them.

Antibiotics are often produced only when the microbe experiences distress, for example, when the food supply starts to run out. The key to antibiotic production technology is, therefore, to maintain a steady but low rate of nutrient supply that is just sufficient to prevent the culture of microorganisms from dying of starvation and thus stimulate antibiotic production. The difficulty is that there is no way of directly measuring how fast the substrate is being consumed. To arrive at the optimum feeding rate, the biotechnologist must therefore rely on trial and error. If the feeding rate is too fast, the tank slowly fills up or the population becomes too dense. Oxygen supplies run out and the culture dies.

To overcome these problems, biotechnologists use a system known as **cyclic fed batch culture (CFBC)**. In this system, fresh nutrients are added continually at a slow rate and whenever the bioreactor threatens to overflow, a portion of the culture is removed. The yield from a CFBC system is superior to that of a simple batch process. One explanation for this is that the CFBC system simulates what happens when two species of microorganisms meet and compete for the same substrate in their natural environment. If one of them is suitably endowed, it could produce an antibiotic to inhibit or even destroy its competitor. It has been suggested that when the bioreactor is almost full, nutrient availability for the individual cells would be low and growth would be slow. Removing a portion of the culture increases the availability of food for the cells left behind in the culture, allowing them to grow faster and to produce antibiotics as a 'panic response' to an unseen competitor.

Manufacture of penicillin

Penicillin, the best-known antibiotic, is produced by strains of the filamentous mould fungi *Penicillium notatum* and *Penicillium chrysogenum*. It is manufactured by growing a specially selected strain of *P. chrysogenum* in huge fermenters or bioreactors capable of holding 100–200 m³ of culture media using a CFBC process. The liquid medium contains a mixture of glucose and lactose. *Penicillium* grows better on glucose but produces more penicillin on lactose. Optimal yields are obtained after each batch has been cultured for between five and eight days. The thickened broth is then passed through a rotating filter to separate the fungal cells from the liquid medium, which contains the valuable antibiotic. The cells are washed and the filtrate and washings are put through a chemical extractor to concentrate the product. Potassium ions are then added to precipitate the product as the potassium salt of penicillin. When dried, the product is 99.5% pure.

Production of single-cell protein

The term **single-cell protein (SCP)** is used to refer to microbial biomass grown specifically as a source of protein food for humans or animals. The idea behind SCP technology is to exploit the fast growth rates of microorganisms and their ability to grow on a cheap source of nitrogen (like ammonia) and a 'worthless' source of carbon (such as industrial or agricultural wastes) to make proteins that are fit for human or animal consumption.

Consider for example a 450 kg animal, such as a prize beef cow, which is fed by being put to pasture. Such an animal would, in the course of a normal day, put on 0.5 kg in body weight. In comparison, a 450 kg standing crop of soy bean plants would, over the same period of time, produce by photosynthesis an estimated 36 kg of proteins in the form of beans and other plant tissues. A 450 kg mass of actively growing bacterial cells, doubling every three hours would increase to a staggering 115.2 tonnes (1 tonne = 1000 kg) during that 24-hour period. This rapid growth rate makes microorganisms potentially a rich source of protein.

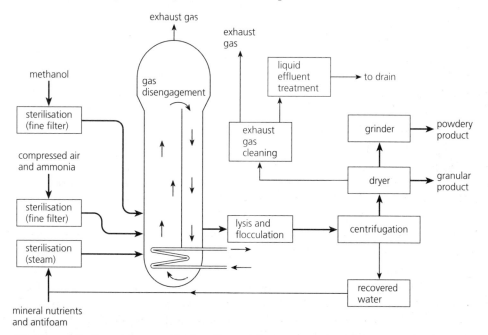

Figure 4.8 The production of Pruteen (single-cell protein)

There are a number of advantages of using microorganisms as a source of protein food. These are:

- their very rapid growth rate
- the high nutritional value of SCP (80% of the dry mass of bacterial cells is protein)
- the ability of microorganisms to feed on cheap or 'worthless' agricultural or industrial wastes as substrates
- the fact that microorganisms are better subjects than plants or animals for large scale screening for qualities like high growth rates, nutritional value, etc. and for genetic manipulation with mutagens such as gamma rays.

ICI developed an SCP plant capable of producing 150 tonnes of dried bacterial biomass per day. It was sited in the North Sea and had a fermentation tower that stood 50 metres tall with a capacity of 1500 m³. A type of bacterium, *Methylophilus methylotrophus*, capable of feeding on methanol as its source of carbon, was chosen for culture. Methanol is a product of natural gas and is readily available in the North Sea. Ammonia was supplied as a cheap source of nitrogen for the bacteria. The plant was built as a continuous process with bacterial biomass being continually harvested and replaced by an equivalent quantity of fresh and recycled media. The product was marketed under the trade name Pruteen as an animal feed.

Despite the huge potential, SCP technology has not had a major impact on global protein supplies. There are several reasons for this.

- Most people find the idea of eating microbes not very appealing.
- The meat from animals fed on SCP was reported to have an unpleasant taste and smell.
- There was a persistent suspicion that oil-derived carbon substrates used for SCP production contained traces of **carcinogens** (cancer-causing substances).
- Due to increased world soybean production and overproduction of milk in Europe, SCP projects were found to be only marginally economic.

ICI stopped producing Pruteen for economic reasons in 1985.

Production of mycoprotein

A food protein made from microorganisms that is used in a range of food products for human consumption is **mycoprotein**. It is made from the hyphae of a filamentous fungus called *Fusarium graminearum*. The fungus is cultured on a solution of glucose prepared from cereal starch (carbon source), ammonia (nitrogen source), mineral salts and choline (promotes longer hyphal growth).

A special type of fermenter known as an **air-lift fermenter** is used for culturing the fungus. The fermenter is built like loop and has two main parts: a **riser** and a **downcomer**. The liquid medium circulates between the two parts, driven by air pumped in through a sparger at the bottom of the riser. The air makes the freshly aerated parts of the liquid medium less dense thus causing it to rise. A **gas separator** at the top of the riser removes gases bubbling out of the liquid, thus preventing the gases from being sucked into the downcomer. This leaves the air-depleted parts of

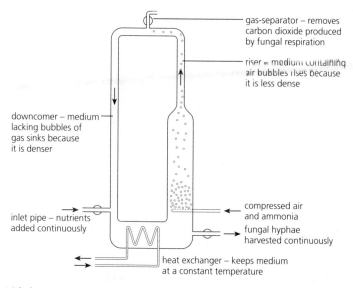

gas-separator – removes carbon dioxide produced by fungal respiration

riser = medium containing air bubbles rises because it is less dense

downcomer – medium lacking bubbles of gas sinks because it is denser

inlet pipe – nutrients added continuously

compressed air and ammonia

fungal hyphae harvested continuously

heat exchanger – keeps medium at a constant temperature

Figure 4.9 An airlift fermenter for the continuous culture of *Fusarium graminearum* for the production of mycoprotein

the liquid more dense causing it to sink. A stirrer, which would break up the long, delicate hyphae, is therefore not required. The culture is maintained at 30 °C to promote an optimum rate of growth. A system of continuous culture is used with fresh, sterile nutrients being added at a constant rate and an equivalent quantity of fungal hyphae being removed for processing.

Rapidly dividing cells contain high levels of ribonucleic acid (RNA) that need to be reduced to meet World Health Organization guidelines for human consumption. This is done by heating the culture to 64 °C. Protein-digesting enzymes are denatured at this temperature but not those enzymes that break down ribosomal RNA. RNA-digesting enzymes break down the RNA to nucleotides that then diffuse out of the fungal hyphae into the spent medium, thus leaving the hyphae with a reduced RNA content. The hyphae are then spread over a moving filter and much of the liquid is removed by vacuum treatment. Finally, natural flavourings such as vegetable extracts, rehydrated egg white and whey proteins may be added to make the product more appealing.

Mycoprotein is visually more acceptable for eating because the fungal hyphae resemble myofibrils in muscle tissue. People are also less put off when told that the product was cultured on potato starch rather than on petroleum waste. In Britain, the product is marketed under the name of Quorn.

Questions

6 What is an air-lift fermenter? What are the advantages of this type of fermenter as compared to a standard bioreactor?

7 Give two advantages and two disadvantages of culturing microorganisms as a source of protein food compared to the farming of animals.

8 What are mycoproteins and explain how the RNA content of mycoproteins is reduced.

Examination questions

1 The diagram shows an industrial fermenter.

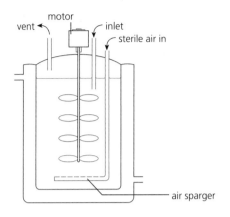

a Suggest how
  i) the air is sterilised before it is allowed to enter the fermenter,
  ii) the fermenter is sterilised between fermentations. (2)
b What is the function of the vent? (1)
c i) Explain why there are difficulties in maintaining the temperature of a large industrial fermenter.
  ii) How is maintenance of temperature achieved in this fermenter? (2)

(total = 5)

NEAB, June 1995

2 The diagram below shows the sequence of processes involved in the brewing of beer.

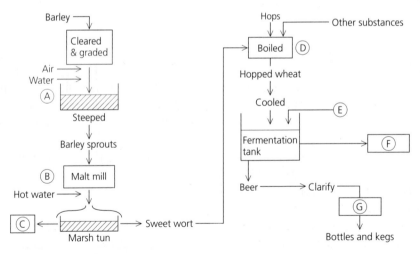

a Describe the changes occurring in the barley grains in the vessel labelled A. (2)
b The malt mill (B) dries and crushes the barley sprouts. State *one* effect this has on the sequence of processes. (1)
c The nutrient-rich liquor is called sweet wort. Suggest *one* use for the residues which have been separated from the liquor and removed at C. (1)

d Suggest *one* substance the brewer might add to the mash in order to get a low-carbohydrate or 'lite' beer. (1)

e Suggest *one* reason why the sweet wort is boiled at D. (1)

f i) Identify E which is added to the fermentation tank to produce beer. (1)

ii) Describe exactly what is happening in the fermentation tank to produce beer. (3)

g i) Give the economic importance of *one* product removed at F. (1)

ii) State one further process which the beer undergoes at G and explain why this is necessary. (2)

(total = 13)

ULEAC, June 1992

3 The diagrams below show the sequence in the process of bulk (long) fermentation commonly used for breadmaking.

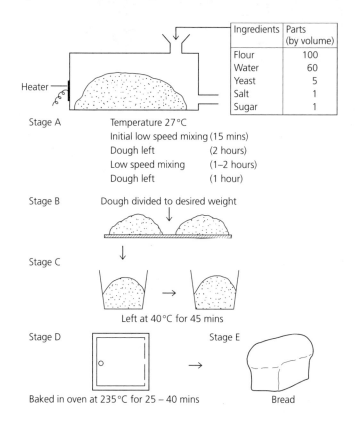

Ingredients	Parts (by volume)
Flour	100
Water	60
Yeast	5
Salt	1
Sugar	1

Heater

Stage A

Temperature 27 °C
Initial low speed mixing (15 mins)
Dough left (2 hours)
Low speed mixing (1–2 hours)
Dough left (1 hour)

Stage B   Dough divided to desired weight

Stage C

Left at 40 °C for 45 mins

Stage D   Stage E

Baked in oven at 235 °C for 25 – 40 mins   Bread

a i) Explain the purpose of the initial low speed mixing during stage A. (2)

ii) Describe the metabolic processes occurring during this stage. (3)

iii) Give one reason for maintaining the temperature at 27 °C during this stage. (1)

b i) Explain the effect of increasing the temperature to 40 °C during this stage. (2)

ii) Explain the effect of increasing the temperature to 235 °C during baking (stage D). (1)

(total = 9)

ULEAC, June 1994

4 Below is a photograph of a fungus *Fusarium graminearum*, used in the manufacture of mycoprotein.

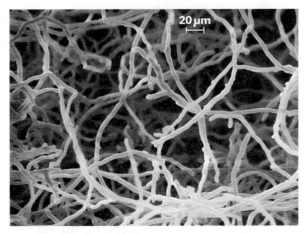

a i) Identify the structure labelled S. (1)

   ii) State a function for S. (1)

   iii) State the magnification of the photograph. Show your working. (1)

Below is a flow diagram for the production of mycoprotein by continuous culture. The fermenter is of a type known as an air lift fermenter. Air is bubbled into the fermenter to supply sterile oxygen. The products of fermentation are harvested in a centrifuge.

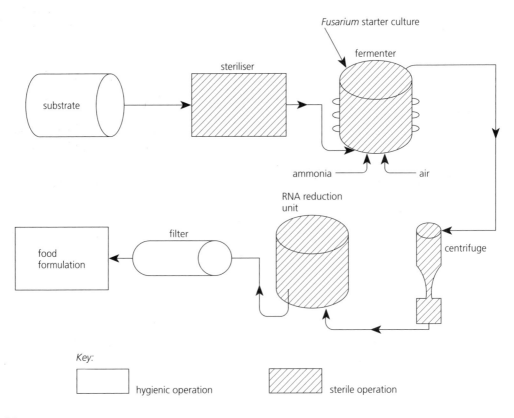

b i) Explain why the production of mycoprotein must take place under sterile conditions. (2)

ii) Explain the term *continuous culture*. (2)

iii) Suggest why ammonia is required by *Fusarium graminearum*. (1)

iv) State **two** functions of the air in the fermenter. (2)

v) Explain the use of the centrifuge in the production of the mycoprotein. (1)

vi) Explain why the RNA content of the mycoprotein is reduced. (1)

c State **two** ways in which mycoprotein is modified during the food formulation process. (2)

The table shows a comparison of the major nutrients in mycoprotein and beef.

Nutrient	Dry mass/percent	
	Mycoprotein	**Beef**
protein	40–45	60–65
fat	10–15	30–40
mineral salts	3–4	1–2
fibre	30–40	none

d With reference to the table, state **two** advantages of using mycoprotein as a meat substitute. (2)

e Suggest **two** reasons why the public might be reluctant to substitute mycoprotein for beef even though it may be better for their diet. (2)

(total = 18)

UCLES, June 1995

Suggestions for learning experiences

Activity 5.6 The production of yoghurt (Investigation) *Advanced Biology Study Guide*, CG Clegg and DG Mackean with PH Openshaw and RC Reynolds. John Murray (Publishers) Ltd 1996, page 73.

Activity 5.7 Building and testing a fermenter (Investigation) *Advanced Biology Study Guide*, CG Clegg and DG Mackean with PH Openshaw and RC Reynolds. John Murray (Publishers) Ltd 1996, page 74.

Activity 5.9 Commercially available rennins compared (Investigation) *Advanced Biology Study Guide*, CG Clegg and DG Mackean with PH Openshaw and RC Reynolds. John Murray (Publishers) Ltd 1996, page 76.

Work Card 7 Microbes and breadmaking *Practical Microbiology and Biotechnology for Schools*, Paul Wymer. Macdonald Educational 1987.

5 Genetic manipulation

Wild-type microorganisms, that is free-living ones, are adapted to survive (by natural selection) in their natural surroundings. They are not adapted to produce large quantities of a substance that happens to be desired by humans. Biologists, however, have developed a variety of techniques that can be used to modify microorganisms into highly efficient workers in the service of humankind.

Isolation and selection

The oldest of these techniques is **isolation** as pure cultures followed by **selection** and purposeful culture of the best strains for the required task.

Inducing mutations

Another technique consists of **inducing mutations** by exposing useful strains of microorganisms to mutagenic chemicals such as mustard gas or to X-rays, γ-rays or ultraviolet radiation. The mutagenic chemicals or radiation damage DNA thus producing a change in the structure of a gene known as a **mutation**. Mutagens hit genes at random. They rarely produce microorganisms with new properties or new functions. Instead, mutations tend to result in a loss of a particular characteristic or function. Consider, for example, a sequence of reactions involving two enzymes, 1 and 2, that catalyse the conversion of substance A to substance B to substance C as summarised in the equation below:

$$A \quad \overset{\text{enzyme 1}}{\Rightarrow} \quad B \quad \overset{\text{enzyme 2}}{\Rightarrow} \quad C$$

If enzyme 2 is defective because the gene that codes for it has been damaged, the mutant organism would not be able to convert substance B to substance C. Substance B would accumulate and diffuse out of the cytoplasm into the surrounding medium. Such an organism may not survive in nature but substance B might just happen to be what the industrial microbiologist is looking for.

Inducing mutations is often a rewarding procedure. Improvements in yield of as much as 200–300 times have been reported. Virtually all industrial strains of micro-organisms are mutants and their productivities are closely guarded industrial secrets.

Somatic cell hybridisation

Somatic (body) cell hybridisation involves the fusion of two body cells to produce a single hybrid cell possessing the genetic information of the two original cells. It is a technique that makes possible the shuffling of genes between sexually incompatible species. However, before plant, bacterial or fungal cells can be fused, their cell walls will need to be removed; this is because the cell wall acts as a physical and chemical barrier. Removal of the cell walls is achieved by putting the cells in a solution containing a combination of digestive enzymes (e.g. cellulases, pectinases, etc.). The enzymes dissolve the cell wall, thus leaving a naked cell surrounded only by its plasma membrane. Such naked cells are very fragile and are known as **protoplasts**.

When incubated, protoplasts can regrow cell walls.

Bacterial, fungal or plant protoplasts or animal cells can be induced to fuse in one of three ways:

1 One method puts the cells next to each other and then exposes them to a **strong electric field**.
2 Another method makes use of a chemical polymer called **ethane-1,2-diol** (formerly known as **polyethylene glycol**). It promotes cell fusion by binding into lipid membranes.
3 The last method makes use of some types of **viruses** that have lipid envelopes and gain entry by fusing with the cell membrane of the host cell. If the virus simultaneously fuses with two cells, it effectively joins them via a narrow membranous bridge.

The product of cell fusion is known as a **somatic hybrid**. At first the hybrid cell has two nuclei, each containing the chromosomes of one of the parent cells. Later, during cell division, the nuclear membranes disintegrate and a new, single nuclear membrane forms enclosing both sets of chromosomes.

Somatic cell hybridisation is used in the manufacture of monoclonal antibodies (see Chapter 8) and in plant breeding programmes to produce hybrid plants with desirable characteristics of two different types of plants.

Genetic engineering

By far the most powerful tool available to biotechnologists is **genetic engineering**: a variety of techniques that enable microbiologists to take a gene from one organism and to transfer it into another. A gene from a plant cell, for example, could in theory be cut out and inserted into an animal cell and vice versa. The benefits arising out of genetic engineering include cows that produce pharmaceuticals in their milk, bacteria that make human insulin, tomatoes that are tastier and that remain firm longer, potatoes that are pest resistant and so on.

Production of human insulin

How does one get bacteria to produce human insulin or any other protein alien to the bacteria? Answer – in four main steps:

1 getting copies of the desired gene
2 attaching the desired gene to a plasmid
3 getting harmless bacteria to take up the plasmids
4 identifying the bacterial clones that are producing the foreign protein.

Isolating the human insulin gene

All human cells have a copy of the gene that codes for human insulin. It is, however, only one amongst tens of thousands of other genes carried on the chromosomes. To try to locate and then extract it would be like searching for a needle in a haystack.

Using reverse transcriptase

Genetic engineers have a bag of tools, so to speak, one of which is an enzyme called **reverse transcriptase**. This enzyme is extracted from retroviruses and it catalyses the conversion of RNA to DNA. Insulin is a hormone secreted in large quantities by the beta cells of the islets of Langerhans in the pancreas. A high proportion of the RNA in such cells should therefore consist of mRNA for insulin synthesis. If the genetic engineer adds reverse transcriptase to a test tube containing RNA extracted from human beta cells, he or she will end up with a test tube of DNA, a high proportion of which will be the gene for human insulin.

Attaching the human insulin gene to a plasmid

Genetic engineers have three other important tools at their disposal. These are

1 restriction enzymes
2 DNA ligases
3 plasmids.

(It is now possible to purchase purified reverse transcriptase, restriction enzymes, DNA ligases and plasmids from companies that specialise in marketing them.)

Restriction endonucleases

Restriction endonucleases are enzymes that nearly all bacteria possess. These enzymes can recognise alien DNA and cut it up. Bacteria use them to defend themselves against viral attack. Genetic engineers use them like a pair of molecular scissors, so that the desired gene can be cut out and spliced into a carrier molecule that will then transport the alien gene into a chosen bacterium. These enzymes were so named because it was discovered that viruses grown on certain strains of the colon bacterium *Escherichia coli*, were restricted in their ability to grow on other strains. It was later discovered that these other strains possess enzymes for cutting up the viral DNA. The term 'endonuclease' refers to the fact that the cut occurs between two nucleotides within the DNA molecules as opposed to enymes called 'exonucleases', which cut off nucleotides from the ends of the DNA molecules.

Many hundreds of restriction enzymes have been extracted from bacteria. Each type recognises a specific short sequence of nucleotides (the building units of nucleic acids) and breaks the phosphodiester bond between two nucleotides. For example, the restriction enzyme *Eco*RI, extracted from *E. coli*, recognises the sequence of bases GAATTC. It cuts DNA whenever this sequence appears. The break occurs at slightly different points on the two strands of DNA, leaving each fragment with a short, single-stranded end which is complementary to the end on the other fragment. These single-stranded ends are 'sticky' in the sense that they will adhere to each other by hydrogen bonding if brought together. If DNA fragments from two different organisms cut by the same restriction enzyme are mixed in a test tube, their matching sticky ends will attract one another, thus connecting the two fragments together. This process is known as **annealing**.

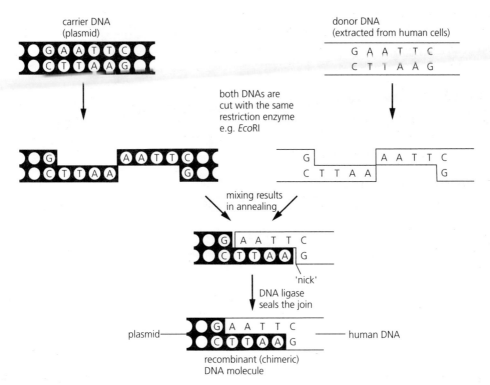

Figure 5.1 Procedure for constructing a recombinant DNA molecule

Some restriction enzymes recognise a sequence of three or four bases. Others recognise longer sequences consisting of six or seven bases. The three-to-four-base-cutters will generally yield short DNA fragments whereas the six-to-seven-base-cutters will generally yield longer pieces of DNA. This is because a specific sequence of six or seven bases occurs relatively infrequently whereas the same cannot be said for a specific sequence of three or four bases. Long DNA fragments are, in general, more useful to genetic engineers than short ones because they are likely to carry whole or intact genes.

DNA ligases

All living organisms possess enzymes called **DNA ligases**. They use them to make and repair DNA. Genetic engineers use them to join newly annealed DNA fragments to form **hybrid** or **recombinant molecules**.

Plasmids

Most bacteria carry plasmids – small, circular pieces of DNA that are quite separate from the bacterial chromosome. Genetic engineers use plasmids as **vectors** to transfer genes into bacteria.

Making recombinant DNA

Having obtained copies of the human insulin gene, the next task is to splice the insulin gene into a plasmid that will carry the alien gene into a bacterium. This is done by choosing a suitable restriction enzyme and then adding it to a test tube

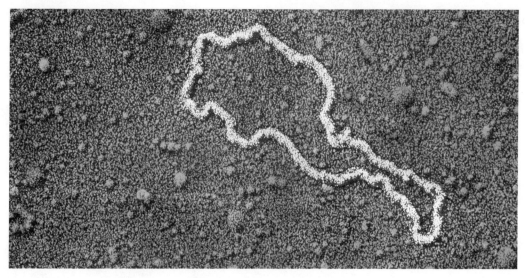

Figure 5.2 A scanning electron micrograph of a plasmid (×124 000)

containing purified plasmids. The effect is to cut the plasmid circles open, leaving sticky ends on the molecules which are now linear. The same restriction enzyme is then used to cut the human insulin gene, leaving sticky ends. The contents of the two test tubes are mixed. The sticky ends of the two types of DNA adhere and the plasmids reconstitute themselves into circular molecules. Some of the plasmids will hopefully have an alien gene inserted into them. These are known as **chimeral** or **recombinant plasmids.** DNA ligase is then added to seal the joints between the two types of DNA.

Getting the plasmids into E. coli

The next step consists of inserting the recombinant plasmids into plasmid-free bacteria. Ordinarily DNA cannot pass through cell walls or cell membranes. Biologists, however, have discovered a technique for making bacteria capable of absorbing recombinant plasmids from their environment. It involves adding ice-cold calcium chloride solution to a test tube containing the recombinant plasmids, followed by E. coli, and then incubating the test tube in crushed ice for 15 minutes. The test tube is then immediately immersed in a 42 °C water bath for 90 seconds. The sudden heat treatment shocks the bacteria (or at least some of them) into taking up plasmids from their environment. Those that take up DNA from their surroundings are said to be **transformed**.

Plasmids carry commands in a special sequence of bases known as the **replication origin.** These commands cause bacteria to make copies of the plasmid to pass on to the daughter cells when the bacterium divides. The result is a population consisting of several thousand bacteria each possessing a foreign gene. Genes do not carry such commands. If a gene is not replicated, daughter cells will not acquire the new gene and the genetic engineering exercise would be futile. The term **gene cloning** is used to refer to the isolation and propagation of a specific piece of DNA.

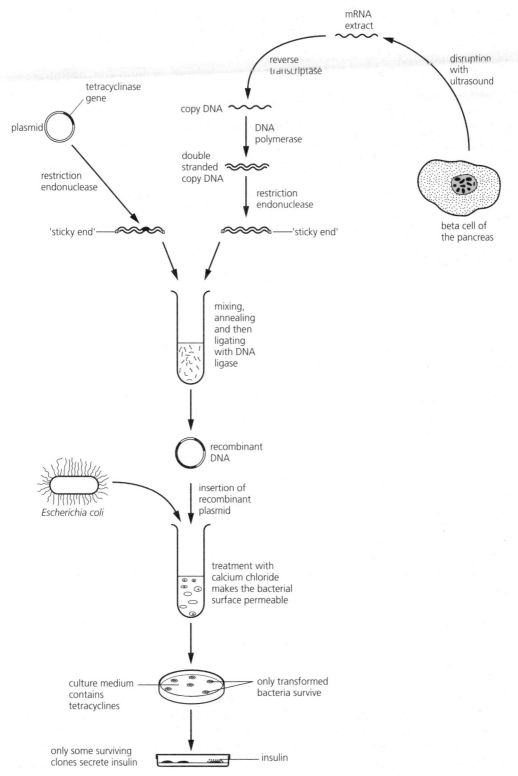

Figure 5.3 The exploitation of bacteria – the insertion of the gene for human insulin in *E. coli*

Identifying the bacterial clones that produce human insulin

How do you distinguish between those bacteria that have taken up plasmids from those that have not? The answer is to start with a plasmid that carries a gene for say ampicillin resistance and spread the bacteria on a culture medium containing ampicillin. Cells that have taken up the plasmid will live whereas those that have not will be killed by the antibiotic.

How do you know which bacteria have picked up plasmids containing the desired gene? The answer is to choose a restriction enzyme that will splice the alien gene into a site occupied by a gene for another antibiotic resistance, say tetracycline resistance. Those that have picked up the desired gene will not be able to produce whatever substance it is that makes them resistant to tetracycline. Such bacteria will be resistant to ampicillin but sensitive to tetracycline.

Not all the transformed, ampicillin resistant but tetracycline sensitive bacteria can, however, be expected to produce human insulin. The reason is that the RNA extracted from the human beta cells consisted of a mixture of RNA molecules, only some of which were mRNA for insulin production.

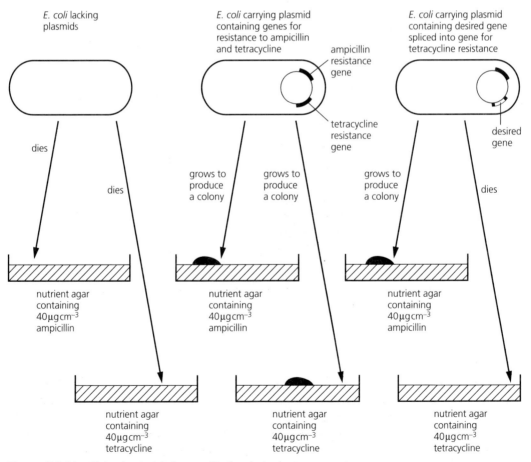

Figure 5.4 Identifying bacterial clones with the desired gene

Making a replica plate

To identify the insulin producers, a plastic disc coated with **anti-insulin antibodies** is placed on to the culture to allow any insulin that is actually produced to bind on to the antibodies. The plastic disc, with the insulin molecules now fixed on to it, is removed and exposed to radioactively labelled antibodies to insulin. If there are any insulin molecules bound on to the disc, the radioactive antibodies will now bind on to them and their presence can be revealed by a technique known as **autoradiography**. It consists of producing an image of a radioactive region by placing the disc on a photographic film and then developing the film. From the position of the spots on the film, you can determine which of the bacterial colonies on the culture plate are actually producing human insulin.

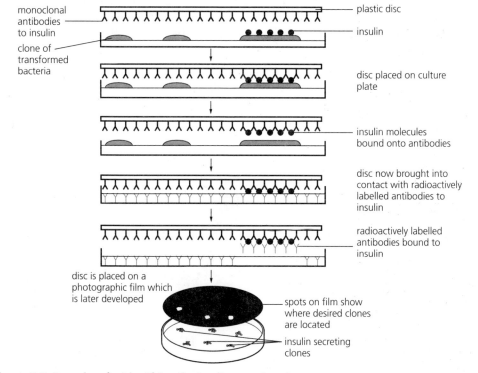

Figure 5.5 Procedure for identifying the insulin-secreting clones

Large-scale culture

The clone that yields the most human insulin is chosen for large-scale culture. It is usually grown as a batch culture in a huge bioreactor. The hormone is later extracted from the spent culture medium and then purified.

An estimated 60 million people worldwide have insulin-dependent diabetes and require daily injections of insulin. The insulin used by people with diabetes was traditionally extracted from the pancreases of pigs or cattle. However, only limited amounts can be obtained from this source. Furthermore, prolonged use of animal insulin does carry a slight risk of allergic reactions, because the body's immune system recognises the substance as a foreign protein and makes antibodies against it.

Human insulin made by recombinant technology is cheaper to produce and available in large quantities. The manufacturers also claim that it is purer. There are, however, reports from some patients that they have become slightly less aware of warning signs of impending hypoglycaemia, such as hunger, sweating and palpitations, after having switched to human insulin.

Questions

1 What are protoplasts?
2 What term is used to describe the role of plasmids in genetic engineering?
3 What name is given to the class of enzymes used by genetic engineers to cut DNA?
4 What are 'sticky ends' and what role do they play in genetic engineering?
5 Give an example of a marker gene and explain its role in genetic engineering.
6 What are replica plates and what are they used for?
7 Give two advantages and one disadvantage of using genetically engineered human insulin compared with traditionally extracted insulin for the treatment of diabetes.

Bovine somatotrophin

Bovine somatotrophin (BST), also known as **bovine growth hormone**, is secreted naturally in tiny quantities by the pituitary gland of the cow. It is a protein and it has three physiological functions:

1 it stimulates growth in young animals
2 it influences carbohydrate and fat metabolism
3 it promotes milk production in lactating cows.

Large quantities of the hormone became available in the late 1970s, when genetic engineers in the United States successfully inserted the BST gene into bacteria. Injected into cows, the protein boosts the milk yield by as much as 20%, partly by increasing the cow's appetite and partly by diverting more of the cow's food intake away from ordinary metabolism and into milk production.

Figure 5.6 Lactating cows injected with bovine somatotrophin (BST) produce up to 20% more milk

What is antisense RNA?

A DNA molecule consists of two linear strands of nucleotides twisted into a double helix. Each nucleotide is made up of a deoxyribose sugar, a phosphate and one of four bases – adenine (A), thymine (T), cytosine (C) or guanine (G). The two strands have an important characteristic – the A on one strand always pairs with T on the other strand, and C with G, as follows:

$$-ATCCGAG-$$
$$-TAGGCTC-$$

The two strands are thus said to be complementary.

RNA differs from DNA in three important ways:

1 it is single stranded
2 its sugar is ribose
3 it has the base uracil (U) where DNA has thymine.

The sequence of bases on messenger RNA (mRNA) spells out the sequence of amino acids that must be strung together to form a protein. Because only one of the two strands of the DNA double helix (known as the **informational strand**) is transcribed into mRNA, the sequence of bases on this strand is said to make sense. The complementary sequence of bases on the other (**non-informational**) strand is said to be **antisense**.

If both the sense and the antisense mRNA are present within the cell, the two complementary strands will bind to each other to form mini, double-stranded helices of RNA. The cell's ribosomes cannot use such double-stranded helices and so no protein is made on the message coded in the gene.

Several countries including the US, the USSR (as it then was), South Africa and Brazil have approved the use of artificially produced BST for improving milk production in cattle. Health fears over drinking the milk produced by cows injected with genetically engineered BST are widely believed to be groundless. BST is in any case present in small quantities in naturally produced milk and, as a protein, it is broken down in the gut.

Critics argue that there may be as yet unknown risks from drinking the milk. They also point to the fact that cows treated with BST suffer a higher incidence of mastitis (inflammation of the udders). They fear that this will cause farmers to use more antibiotics, which will, in due course, reduce the effectiveness of the antibiotics for treating human bacterial diseases. Others accuse the manufacturers of reducing BST-treated cows into unhappy milk-producing machines.

Genetically engineered tomatoes

Most tomatoes are presently picked green to ensure that they are still firm when they arrive in the supermarkets. The green tomatoes are 'ripened' by treatment with a gas called **ethene**, which turns them red but does nothing to develop the flavours associated with fruits that are left to ripen naturally on the plant. Tomatoes turn soft and mushy as they ripen because an enzyme, **polygalacturonase**, breaks down pectin in the cell walls of the tomato cells. To stop the tomatoes from going soft, biotechnologists have devised a way of blocking the production of this enzyme by the tomato cells. They have inserted an artificially synthesised, 'back to front' or **antisense** version of the gene for polygalacturonase. Tomatoes with this gene stay firm longer than traditional tomatoes and can therefore be left to ripen on the plant. The reversed gene (known as the *Flavr Savr* gene) produces **antisense mRNA** that binds on to the mRNA produced by the normal polygalacturonase gene, thus preventing the coding on the normal mRNA from being translated into proteins. The result is tomatoes that are tastier and with a longer shelf-life. The genetically engineered *Flavr Savr* tomato is widely regarded as safe for human consumption. The main reservation centres around the two genes for resistance to antibiotics (kanomycin and neomycin) that were also inserted into the tomato plant. Although these two antibiotics are not used for the treatment of human diseases, there is some concern about the long-term effects of having large amounts of the two antibiotic resistant genes released into the soil by decomposing plant matter.

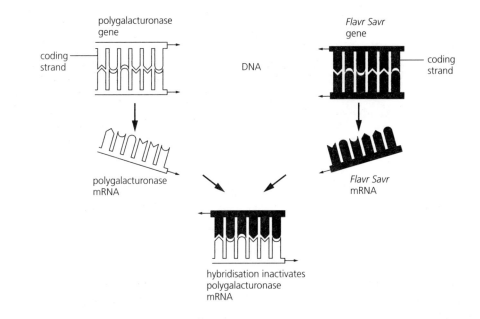

Figure 5.7 Blocking the production of polygalacturonase

How to genetically engineer plants

Among higher organisms, plants are the best candidates for genetic engineering because all nucleated plant cells (unlike mammalian cells) retain the full development potential of the original zygote and are said to be **totipotent**. Small pieces of plant tissue (known as **explants**) or isolated plant cells, when treated in an appropriate way, can grow and give rise to whole plants. Another important consideration is that plants, unlike bacteria, are multicellular organisms. To genetically engineer plants, the alien gene must be inserted in such a way that it enters every cell of the plant. The trick is, therefore, to insert the alien gene not into whole plants but isolated single cells.

Plant cells have robust cell walls and unlike bacterial cells, they cannot be transformed by cold calcium chloride treatment followed by heat shock. There are, however, a number of techniques for getting DNA into plant cells. One method makes use of a particle gun to simply shoot tiny DNA-coated tungsten pellets into plant cells. Another, and still the most widely used technique, makes use of a common soil bacterium, *Agrobacterium tumefaciens*. This bacterium is a natural genetic engineer: it causes **crown gall disease** by transferring a tumour-inducing plasmid into the host plant cells.

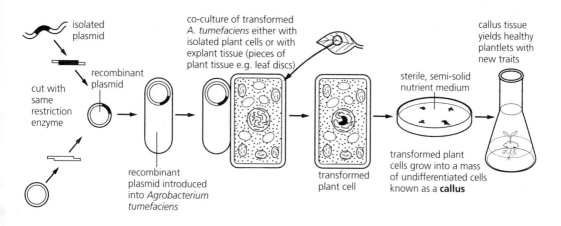

Figure 5.8 Using the bacterium *Agrobacterium tumefaciens* to genetically engineer plants

Before *A. tumefaciens* is used for genetic engineering, however, the tumour-inducing gene needs to be cut out of the plasmid. This process is known as **disarming**. The desired gene along with a marker gene for antibiotic resistance are then spliced into the disarmed plasmid before it is introduced into *A. tumefaciens*. Transformed *A. tumefaciens* bacteria are recognised by their resistance to the antibiotic.

The next step consists of co-culturing the transformed *A. tumefaciens* with isolated plant cells to allow the bacteria to transfer their plasmids into the plant cells. Cells that acquire the plasmid (recognised by the use of a suitable marker gene for plants) are then selected for culture. Given the right physical and chemical conditions (e.g. suitable temperature, pH, range of nutrients, specific plant growth regulators, exclusion of contaminating microorganisms) the cells will divide, grow and give rise to tiny plantlets, which can then be nurtured into healthy **transgenic plants.**

Social, economic and ethical implications

Some public-interest organisations argue that there may be long-term risks from genetic engineering. They fear that a genetically engineered trait may get itself transferred into a crop plant's wild relatives, spread uncontrollably and eliminate other plants lacking those genes. This, they argue, could seriously damage the varied gene pool in wild populations. Supporters of genetic engineering argue that there is no merit in such arguments because the traits in question, such as disease resistance, are already present in the gene pool of wild populations.

There is also the fear that peasant farmers would no longer find it worth while to cultivate local varieties of crop plants but would instead rely on bulk supplies of 'superior' seeds from the big multinational companies such as ICI. This could lead to a serious loss of genetic diversity amongst cultivated crop plants. The UN Food and Agriculture Organization (FAO) reported recently that since 1903, 20 000 varieties of crop plants have been lost in the US and that, in more than 80 countries, there is widespread replacement of local varieties of crop plants with imported, economically superior varieties. It is argued that genetic engineering could make the dwindling genetic diversity crisis worse.

The danger from relying on just a few distinct varieties of crop plants is their vulnerability to disease, pests and severe weather. A new strain of pest or pathogenic fungus, for example, could 'in one step' wipe out a major crop. Refrigerated seed banks have been set up in many countries to conserve threatened seed varieties. Frozen seeds, however, gradually lose their viability and need to be planted out at periodic intervals to regenerate a new harvest of viable seeds. This is not always done as it is labour intensive and therefore costly.

Many small farmers fear that genetic engineering works in favour of the big farmers and that they will gradually be forced out of business. Take BST for example; because of the economics of scale, big farmers will find it more affordable than the small farmer to obtain the veterinary support needed to introduce and manage herds treated with BST. The increased milk production by the big dairies could then make it difficult for the small farmers to survive. The restructuring of agriculture that would follow could then result in unemployment for many farm workers.

Another area of contention concerns the issue of patents (see Chapter 3, page 45). Companies that carry out genetic engineering claim that without the protection of patents it would not be worth their while investing the huge amounts of money needed for research. Farmers, on the other hand, say that patents on genetically engineered crop plants and farm animals threaten their livelihood. The fact is that according to the terms of the patent, seeds or progeny of novel (genetically engineered) plants or animals are not the property of the farmer but the patent holder. A farmer is, therefore, required to pay a royalty whenever a patented plant or animal, or its descendants, produces offspring. A few companies could, as a result, become economically very powerful.

Advances in genetic engineering will also undoubtedly lead eventually to the control of genetic diseases. In time it may even be possible as a matter of routine procedure to take out defective genes and replace them with healthy ones. With that type of technology available, would we then see the day when genes for low intelligence are taken out in exchange for genes for high intelligence? Is it right in the first place for humans to alter the genes of other living organisms, but leave humans alone? Should biotechnologists be allowed to genetically manipulate animals, perhaps even to cause them to suffer physically, to serve the needs of humans? Is the commercial exploitation of life-forms the height of misuse of the environment?

Examination questions

1 The diagrams show the stages by which a bacterial mutant unable to make the essential amino acid tryptophan can be selected with the use of penicillin. Penicillin is an antibiotic which kills growing bacteria only: in the presence of penicillin sensitive bacteria cannot build normal cell walls and burst as the young cells expand.

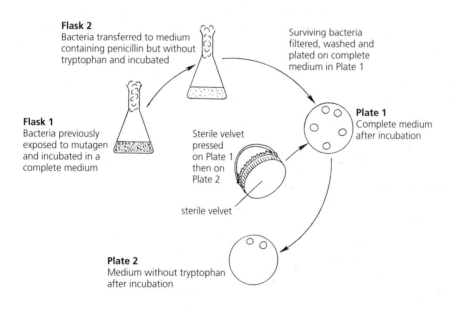

Flask 2
Bacteria transferred to medium containing penicillin but without tryptophan and incubated

Surviving bacteria filtered, washed and plated on complete medium in Plate 1

Flask 1
Bacteria previously exposed to mutagen and incubated in a complete medium

Sterile velvet pressed on Plate 1 then on Plate 2

Plate 1
Complete medium after incubation

sterile velvet

Plate 2
Medium without tryptophan after incubation

a i) What is a mutagen? Give **one** example. (2)
  ii) What is a mutant? (1)
  iii) What is a 'complete medium'? (1)
b i) Suggest why tryptophan is essential to a bacterial cell. (2)
  ii) Using information in the question, explain how this mutant is selected with the use of penicillin. (3)
  iii) Describe the genetic mechanism probably responsible for the mutant unable to make tryptophan. (3)
c Explain the distribution of the colonies after incubation on Plate 2. (3)

d Alexander Fleming discovered penicillin in 1928. It has been said that the mould *Penicillium notatum* contaminated a plate of bacterial colonies resulting in lysis of the bacteria in the region of the mould. A more likely explanation is that Fleming inoculated with bacteria a plate which was already contaminated by *Penicillium notatum*.

i) Why is the first explanation unlikely? (1)

ii) Why is the second explanation more likely? (2)

iii) Draw and label a plate as it would appear after incubation if the second explanation is true. (2)

(total = 20)

AEB, June 1985

2 a Restriction endonuclease enzymes are naturally-occurring proteins which cut DNA molecules into smaller lengths.

i) What is the meaning of the word *restriction* in this context? (1)

ii) What does the term *endonuclease* refer to in connection with the activity of these enzymes? (1)

b i) An endonuclease enzyme called *Hae*III that comes from the bacterium *Haemophilus aegyptius* binds to the sequence GGCC in the 5′ – 3′ direction. It then cuts the double-stranded DNA molecule between G and C nucleotide bases.

By drawing lines, indicate on the sequence below where this enzyme would cut the DNA molecule.

5′ ATAGAATTCGGCCATGAATTCGGCCATA 3′
3′ TATCTTAAGCCGGTACTTAAGCCGGTAT 5′ (1)

ii) Another restriction enzyme called *Eco*R1 that comes from the bacterium *Escherichia coli* binds to the sequence GAATTC, again in the 5′ – 3′ direction. It then cuts the double-stranded DNA molecule between the G and the A nucleotide bases.

By drawing lines, indicate on the sequence below where this enzyme would cut the DNA molecule.

5′ ATAGAATTCGGCCATGAATTCGGCCATA 3′
3′ TATCTTAAGCCGGTACTTAAGCCGGTAT 5′ (1)

c Study the binding sites for the two enzymes carefully.

i) State **one** significant feature that is common to both sequences (1)

ii) State **one** significant feature that is different in the two sequences.(1)

d *Eco*R1 has often been used in genetic engineering.

i) Explain the technical reason why this enzyme has been so popular.(2)

ii) Give the name of one other type of enzyme that is essential in genetic engineering. (1)

e A certain restriction enzyme was used to cut DNA from a pair of homologous male and female chromosomes. The enzyme cut DNA into fragments as shown below, numbered for convenience.

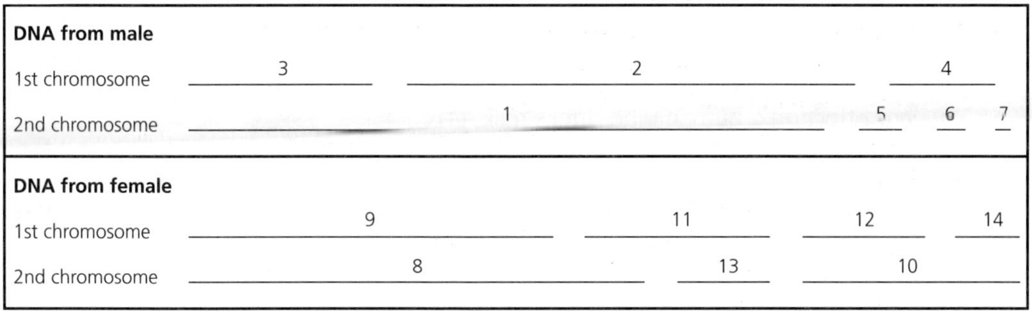

DNA from male						
1st chromosome	3	2		4		
2nd chromosome		1		5	6	7

DNA from female				
1st chromosome	9	11	12	14
2nd chromosome	8	13	10	

The DNA fragments from the male and the female were then separated according to their relative size using the technique of electrophoresis. The pattern of bands for the female resulting from the electrophoresis is shown below.

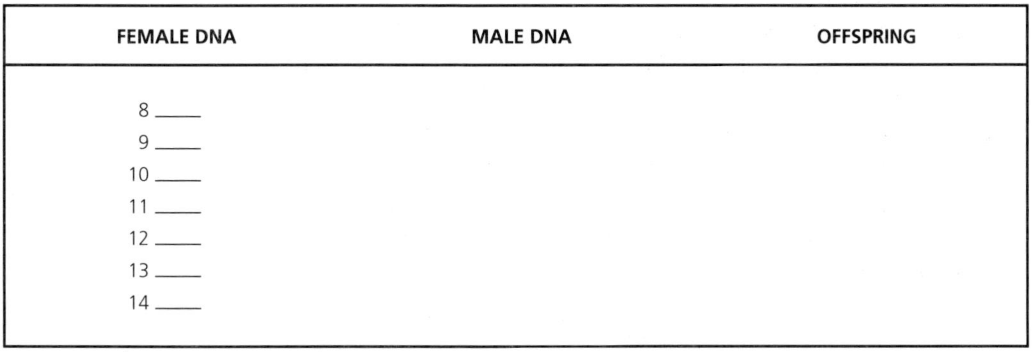

FEMALE DNA	MALE DNA	OFFSPRING
8 ——		
9 ——		
10 ——		
11 ——		
12 ——		
13 ——		
14 ——		

i) On the figure draw and label the male band pattern of DNA in the same manner as already done for the female pattern, using the numbers 1–7.

ii) In the third column of the figure, draw and label one of the possible band patterns for an offspring of a mating between the two parents. (Assume that each chromosome is inherited unchanged).(3)   (total = 12)

O & C, June 1995

3 Bovine somatotrophin, BST, is a hormone which, when given to cows, will increase milk production. BST used for this purpose is made by genetic engineering. The process is summarised below:

The BST gene is isolated from the DNA of a cow

⇓

The BST gene is inserted into a bacterial cell

⇓

The bacterium is cloned and the BST isolated

a Describe how enzymes may be used to isolate the BST gene from the DNA of a cow and insert this gene into the DNA of a bacterial cell. (3)

b BST is a protein. Explain why any BST that gets into the cow's milk will be unlikely to have any effect on a human who drinks milk. (1)

c Suggest why cows that are being treated with BST require extra calcium and protein in their diet. (2)

(total = 6)

NEAB, June 1995

Suggestions for learning experiences

Activity 29.2 Plant protoplasts (Skills and techniques) *Advanced Biology Study Guide*, CG Clegg and DG Mackean with PH Openshaw and RC Reynolds. John Murray (Publishers) Ltd 1996, page 351.

Activity 29.3 Cloning of plants (Skills and techniques/Investigation) *Advanced Biology Study Guide*, CG Clegg and DG Mackean with PH Openshaw and RC Reynolds. John Murray (Publishers) Ltd 1996, page 353.

Uses of microorganisms in agriculture, pollution control and mining

It has been estimated that about one-third of the world's agricultural crops are destroyed by pests. For the past four decades the main weapon against insect pests has been synthetic chemical pesticides. When the first chemical insecticide came on to the market in the mid-1940s, it decimated the insect pest populations and was promptly hailed as 'the atomic bomb of the insect world'. Farmers, however, were soon discovering that the pests were developing resistance and that they were having to use more and more chemical insecticides on their crops.

There are two main reasons why prolonged exposure to large doses of chemical pesticides leads to the development of pesticide resistance. The first is that the chemical pesticide kills not only the pest but also the pest's **natural enemies**, such as solitary wasps. The second is that among the millions of crop pests that are killed by the insecticide, there are usually just a few individuals that are genetically equipped to withstand the effects of the pesticide. These hardy individuals survive and pass their **genes for pesticide resistance** to their offspring. They in their turn will survive the next onslaught of insecticide sprays and pass their genes for pesticide resistance to their offspring. The few pockets of resistant individuals would, in time, spread to areas vacated by susceptible individuals. A few seasons later, the farmer discovers that the entire plantation of crops is once again under threat but this time by an army of individuals resistant to the pesticide. The attack is also much more severe because the natural enemies of the pests are no longer available to keep the pest populations in check. In desperation, the farmer switches to another hopefully more powerful but probably more expensive chemical pesticide.

Today, there are over 800 species of insects that are resistant to at least one insecticide and there are a few so-called 'superbugs' that are resistant to the whole arsenal of chemical pesticides available to the modern farmer.

Chemical pesticides used in ignorance can also be a health hazard. A recent study showed that rice farmers in the Philippines were twice as likely to suffer from respiratory and kidney ailments, and five times as likely to have eye problems if they used chemical pesticides to spray on their crops. The fact is that many farmers in the Philippines cannot afford protective clothing or are disinclined to use it due to the hot tropical weather.

Another drawback with some chemical pesticides is that they take a long time to decompose either by biological or by other natural chemical methods. Chemical pesticides are also mostly fat-soluble substances and, after ingestion, are not easily excreted but tend instead to accumulate in fatty tissues. The result is that the chemical pesticide passes through the food chain becoming more and more concentrated as it proceeds from one life form to another. The top carnivores, for example birds of prey, are thus put at risk, even though the pesticide to start with was low in concentration. The disruption of delicately balanced food webs can often lead to yet more problems with insect pests.

Microbial insecticides

Biologists have discovered several types of soil microorganisms that produce proteins which are highly toxic to insects pests but harmless to humans, wildlife and beneficial arthropods, including wasps and spiders. The best known of these **microbial insecticides** is a bacterium called *Bacillus thuringiensis* (Bt). It produces several types of proteins during spore formation and these are toxic to insect pests. One type of **Bt toxin** specifically kills butterfly and moth caterpillars, another type kills beetles, including the notorious Colorado beetle, and yet another kills fly and mosquito larvae. The microbial insecticide is applied in the same way as a chemical pesticide by spraying a culture of Bt spores in powder form or as a viscous suspension. The Bt toxins kill the target insects by perforating their gut wall, thus allowing the contents of the gut to leak out into the body.

Figure 6.1 The effect of microbial insecticides: the plants on the left have not been sprayed but those on the right have been sprayed with *B. thuringiensis* toxin

Figure 6.2 The genetically engineered tomato plant on the left has the gene for the Bt toxin and is resistant to insect pests. The insect-eaten plant on the right is a normal tomato plant

An important advantage of microbial insecticides over chemical pesticides is that the former is **species specific**, that is, it does not harm other forms of life. The toxins, being protein, also break down rapidly leaving no environmentally harmful residues.

In recent years, genetic engineers have succeeded in inserting the Bt toxin gene into a number of crop plants, thus enabling the plants to produce their own Bt toxin. Pests that feed on these transgenic plants eat the toxin and die. The much hoped for no-spray crop plant has indeed become a reality – or so it is hoped.

Many scientists, however, have been critical of this new development. They warn that the arrival of Bt-producing crop plants could hasten the evolution of resistance to the Bt toxin. Recent reports from southern USA that cotton plants, genetically engineered to produce their own Bt toxin, have succumbed to attack by the cotton bollworm, are clearly disturbing new developments.

Most pest control experts favour the use of Bt toxins as part of an **integrated pest management (IPM) programme**. They argue that pest populations are best kept under control not with a single 'killer punch' but with a series of 'small blows' involving crop rotation, altered dates of planting to avoid peak periods of pest development, biological control using natural enemies and sparing use of Bt toxins and other pesticides. In this way, the development of resistance to the pesticides could be forestalled.

Questions

1 What are microbial insecticides?
2 State two advantages of microbial insecticides over chemical insecticides.

Rhizobial inocula for plant nodulation

An important dogma in biology is the law of limiting factors. It states that the growth of an organism is limited by the availability of whatever nutrient is the scarcest. For plant growth, the element most commonly in short supply is nitrogen. Nitrogen is an essential constituent of proteins, nucleic acids and many other molecules that make up the body of living organisms. There is plenty of nitrogen in the air but plants and animals cannot make use of atmospheric nitrogen because it is an inert gas.

A type of soil bacteria called *Rhizobium* possesses an enzyme called **nitrogenase**, which enables it to 'fix' the nitrogen in the air to form ammonium ions (NH_4^+) and thus make use of this abundant source of nitrogen. To do this, individual bacteria of the *Rhizobium* species must first infect the roots of the leguminous plant and induce the infected root to form swellings called **nodules.** The bacteria divide repeatedly within the root nodules and then change into dormant forms capable of converting atmospheric nitrogen into ammonium ions.

The association between *Rhizobium* and the leguminous plant is one of mutual benefit and is said to be **symbiotic**. The plant provides the bacteria with a ready supply of food (e.g. sugars and amino acids) and it gets in return ammonium ions, which it uses as raw materials for protein and nucleic acid synthesis. If properly exploited, this symbiotic association can be of great value to agriculture.

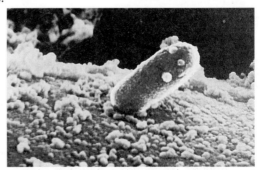

Figure 6.3 *Rhizobium*, a nitrogen-fixing bacterium, attaches itself to a root hair of a leguminous plant

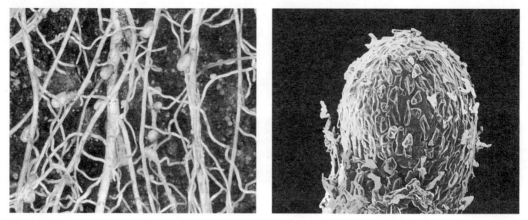

Figure 6.4 Root nodules of leguminous plants; and a close-up of a root nodule (×15)

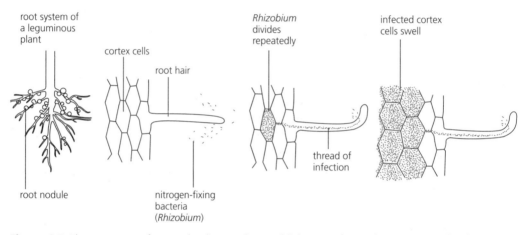

Figure 6.5 The sequence of events leading to the establishment of a symbiotic relationship between *Rhizobium* and a leguminous plant

Promoting nitrogen fixation

One agricultural practice that has proved very successful in India and Nigeria is **alley cropping**. It consists of planting nitrogen-fixing shrubs in rows between non-nodulating crop plants.

Another useful agricultural practice is to **inoculate the seeds** of leguminous plants with a selected strain of *Rhizobium* with a view to ensuring good nodulation of the developing root systems of the crop plants. The usual procedure is to introduce the bacteria as a coating over the seeds or as a peat-based inoculum, which is drilled into the soil together with the seeds at the time of sowing. In the first method, the selected rhizobial culture is mixed with finely ground calcium carbonate and a binding agent such as gum arabic. The mixture is then applied as a coating or pellet on the seeds. In the second method, the inoculum is sprayed on to sterilised, finely divided peat or compost, which is then left to mature for 48 hours before packaging. If the final product is not too moist, the bacteria will remain viable for up to a year if stored at 4 °C.

A much more ambitious project is to genetically engineer non-leguminous crop plants such as maize or wheat to enable them to 'fix' atmospheric nitrogen. There is still a lot of research that needs to be done but the task is expected to be accomplished almost certainly within the next few decades.

Silage production

Silage consists of pickled forage crops, such as grass, sugar beet tops and whole crop cereals, that are cut or harvested in the green state and preserved in succulent form, under acid conditions, for later use as animal feedstuffs. It is made in walled pits or tall towers called **silos**.

Ruminant livestock, for example breeding herds of cattle, are to a large extent fed by being put to pasture. Stored feedstuffs come into use when grazing is not possible during the severe months of winter. Almost any forage crop can be ensilaged. The basic principle in silage-making is fermentation by bacteria of the carbohydrates in the plant material to organic acids and proteins to amino acids.

Desirable and undesirable bacteria

Two categories of bacteria, one desirable and the other undesirable, control the fermentation of carbohydrates in silos. Both types are present in the soil and on crop plants. The desirable bacteria convert carbohydrates anaerobically to **lactic acid**. They belong to two genera, *Lactobacillus* and *Streptococcus*. The undesirable bacteria are of two main types. One type, a species of *Clostridium*, is an obligate anaerobe and it converts carbohydrates to butanoic acid. The other type consists of aerobic bacteria of decay, which degrade carbohydrates to carbon dioxide and water.

Making silage

To make silage, forage crops are cut ideally after a period of dry sunny weather when photosynthesis and wilting would produce conditions that favour high sugar concentration within the plant tissues. The cut crop may also be mechanically lacerated to promote wilting. If the crop is wet, the organic acids produced during fermentation will not be concentrated enough to lower the pH to below the 4.0 level needed to suppress the activities of the *Clostridia*.

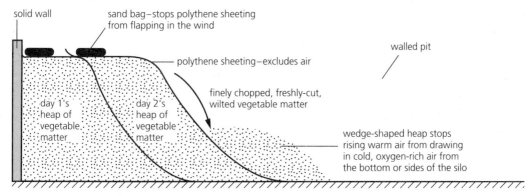

Figure 6.6 The making of silage in silos

Assuming that the cut crop is high in sugar and its moisture content is no higher than 65%, the green finely chopped vegetable matter is heaped into a silo and then covered with polythene sheeting to exclude air. For the first few hours, the living plant cells respire aerobically, consuming oxygen and thus creating conditions that increasingly favour the growth of anaerobic lactic acid bacteria, which multiply rapidly. These bacteria feed on the carbohydrates breaking them down to lactic acid.

Lactic acid is a relatively strong acid. Its rapid production lowers the pH of the ensiling material, thus creating conditions that inhibit the lactic acid bacteria as well as other species of bacteria.

Well-made silage is light-brown in colour. It has a sharp taste, little smell and it contains lactic acid. It is very stable and will keep for years if air is excluded. Poorly made silage is dull olive-green in colour with a rancid smell. It contains butanoic acid and will not keep for more than a few months. It is unpalatable to livestock.

Questions

3 What is silage?

4 Explain why silage is best made after a spell of dry sunny weather.

Straw and stubble digestion

Straw is the dry cut stalk of the cereal plant and stubble is the lower end of grain-stalks left in the ground after harvest. Approximately 10 million tonnes of straw are produced on British farms each year. About 40% of this is baled and removed for use in a variety of ways. Most commonly, the straw is used as bedding for farm animals as it readily absorbs urine and dung. The mushroom and paper industries are also important users of baled straw.

Where there is no demand for the straw, burning was a widely practised method of disposal. However, the burning of straw came under frequent public condemnation because of the accompanying smoke pollution and also because it was widely regarded as a wasteful practice which added to the 'greenhouse effect'. Since 1990, a European Law has been in force banning the burning of straw. The ban is expected to benefit agriculture in an indirect way by increasing the earthworm population since earthworms feed on organic residues left on the soil.

Earthworms improve the soil in a number of ways:

- by pulling leaves from the soil surface into their burrows, they help to increase the organic content of the soil without damaging soil structure
- their burrows help aerate the soil
- their burrows also improve soil drainage, promote water retention (important during the dry summer months) and reduce soil erosion by allowing rainwater to penetrate swiftly into the root layer instead of running over the soil surface and washing away soil particles
- worm casts enrich the soil with valuable minerals and useful microorganisms.

In contrast to the gentle and beneficial activities of earthworms, ploughing the surplus straw into soil has few advantages and several disadvantages. The main advantage is that straw incorporation does improve soil texture and soil drainage. However, it can have disastrous results. Deep within the soil, because of the anaerobic conditions, the organic matter decomposes only partially, remaining as a fibrous mass. In most cases, the partially decomposed material absorbs minerals from the surrounding soil and is toxic to the roots of the next crop. It can also lead to greatly increased slug and snail populations, resulting in the enhanced use of chemical pesticides.

Stubble and straw contain phosphate and potassium but little nitrogen. They are said to have high C : N (carbon to nitrogen) ratios. For maize stubble, the C : N ratio is 30 : 1. If bacteria of decay are to utilise all the carbon available in stubble and straw, they will need to obtain **extra nitrogen** from the surrounding soil to satisfy their own relatively low C : N ratios. Assimilation of inorganic nutrients by microorganisms during decomposition is known as **immobilisation**. Ploughing to incorporate straw before planting, could, therefore, lead to immobilisation of the mineral nitrogen and consequent nitrogen deficiency of the crop plants.

When bacteria are eaten by other soil organisms, such as protozoa, some of the carbon in the dead bacteria will be released as carbon dioxide by the respiring assimilating organisms. The relatively low C : N ratio of bacterial matter will now lead to an excess of nitrogen relative to carbon. Part of the nitrogen in the bacterial substrate will be released as ammonium ions into the soil. The release of inorganic minerals during decomposition is known as **mineralisation**. When land is ploughed in the autumn, the increased availability of air will result in a sudden flush of mineralisation from the disturbed organic matter. This can lead to leaching of nitrate (formed from ammonia) and its eventual entry into water supplies.

Converting straw into ethanol

A recent development is the use of genetically engineered, thermophilic (heat-loving) bacteria for converting straw, corn cobs and other vegetable matter into **ethanol**. The genetically engineered bacteria converts 30% more plant material into ethanol than yeast, the microorganism traditionally chosen for such fermentation processes. This is because the bacterium possesses enzymes for breaking down **hemicellulose**, a major constituent of plant cell walls, which yeast cells cannot digest. The heat produced during the fermentation process keeps the fermenter at around 70 °C. Ethanol vaporises at this temperature and is drawn off continuously by mild vacuum suction and then condensed into a liquid. Farmers can sell the product or use it as a fuel additive to petrol.

The Brazilian gasohol programme

When in 1972 the oil-producing nations (OPEC) raised the price of crude oil quite dramatically to regulate its production, they caused a number of countries with no fossil fuel reserves to look very seriously at ways of producing an alternative fuel to petrol. In 1975, a government-sponsored programme was set up in Brazil to produce **ethanol** by fermentation of cane sugar followed by **distillation** to the anhydrous liquid. Brazil today has four million cars running on ethanol and a further million running on **gasohol**, a mixture of 20% ethanol and 80% gasoline (petrol).

Figure 6.7 The best distilleries in the world. These Brazilian sugar factories convert the juice of the sugar cane plant into ethanol for use as a petrol substitute

Advantages

- Ethanol is a much 'cleaner' fuel than petrol. Cars running on ethanol produce 20–30% less carbon monoxide, 15% less nitrogen oxides, virtually no sulphur dioxide emissions and their production of carbon dioxide is balanced by absorption for photosynthesis by new sugar cane plants. The overall effect on global warming is therefore zero.
- Ethanol is a lead-free fuel.
- Another benefit is the use of bagasse (the dry pulp left over from the crushing of the sugar cane plant) as animal feed or for burning in high-pressure turbines to produce electricity.
- Biologically produced ethanol also creates thousands of jobs in rural areas.

Figure 6.8 Running on ethanol (alcohol) – a cleaner, renewable fuel

Disadvantages

- Normal petrol engines overheat if run on ethanol and have to be modified. The pistons need strengthening because ethanol has a higher detonation temperature
- To prevent corrosion, the fuel tank also needs to be coated with tin, the fuel pipes with copper and nickel and the carburettor with zinc. All this costs money.
- Fuel consumption is also about 20% heavier for ethanol compared with petrol.

In terms of cost, ethanol at today's prices is more expensive than petrol. However, the world's more easily extractable oil reserves will in the not too distant future become exhausted and crude oil will become harder to extract. The price of petrol, in the medium term, must inevitably rise. Improvements in biotechnology, on the other hand, will lower the cost of ethanol production. Already, Brazil's distilleries are the best in the world. As a further development, Brazilian biologists have recently come up with a genetically engineered yeast that is capable of degrading starch. It has enabled Brazil to extend ethanol production from the sugar cane growing areas to parts of the country where the fast-growing, starch-rich plant cassava is cultivated. This has resulted in a further drop in the production costs of ethanol. Environmentalists also argue that the current price of petrol does not reflect its real cost because it does not fully take into account the cost of the anti-pollution measures that would be needed if petrol is burnt as a fuel.

Questions

5 What is gasohol?
6 Outline the processes involved in the production of bioethanol.
7 Give two advantages and two disadvantages of bioethanol as a fuel for cars compared with petrol.

Production of biogas

Biogas is the name given to methane produced by the anaerobic fermentation of organic waste such as animal dung, sewage sludge or agricultural wastes. It consists of a mixture of 50–80% methane, 15–45% carbon dioxide and about 5% water. The bacteria responsible for forming methane from organic waste are known as **methanogens**. These bacteria are widely distributed in nature but are not commonly encountered because they are **strictly anaerobes** and are killed by exposure to oxygen. They do not, therefore, exist in the open. They are present in marshes, in the black mud at the bottom of ponds and in the rumen of cows.

A covered tank known as a **digester** is used to provide a warm, dark, moist and oxygen-free environment (similar to conditions in a cow's stomach) for the methanogens to produce biogas. Figure 6.9 (overleaf) shows an Indian design for a family-sized digester.

The waste is fed into the digester through an inlet pipe. Fresh cow dung or a sample from a well-established biogas plant is used as a source of methanogens for the plant. The waste is broken down in stages by a cocktail of bacteria. To start with, **saprobiontic bacteria**, which are facultative anaerobes, break down polymer

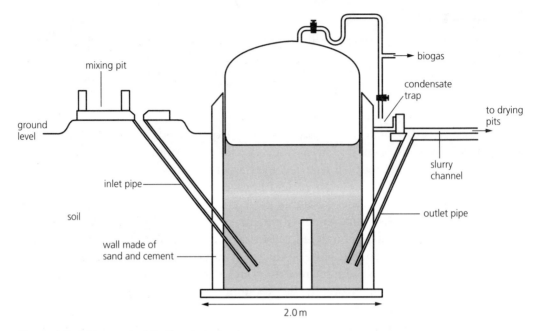

Figure 6.9 A biogas plant (Indian design)

molecules (proteins, fats and polysaccharides) to simpler molecules such as amino acids, fatty acids and sugars. Acid-forming bacteria then break down these monomers to short-chain organic acids, mainly ethanoic and butanoic acids. Some hydrogen and carbon dioxide are also generated. Finally, methane bacteria generate methane gas either by reducing short-chain fatty acids or by combining hydrogen and carbon dioxide.

$$1 \quad CH_3COOH \Rightarrow CH_4 + CO_2$$
$$\quad \text{ethanoic acid} \qquad \text{methane}$$

$$2 \quad CO_2 + 4H_2 \Rightarrow CH_4 + 2H_2O$$

In China and India there are millions of family-sized anaerobic digesters turning out biogas for cooking and lighting. The digesters are commonly built buried in the ground to protect them from extremes of temperature. Glasshouses may also be built on the ground above the biogas plant to provide further insulation against the cold.

Several European towns and cities have in recent years built large-scale biogas plants to convert putricible municipal waste into methane. The biogas produced is used to drive turbines to generate electricity for the local grid. The effluent left behind has few pathogens, a greatly reduced odour and can be processed into compost for use on farms and gardens.

From an environmental point of view, biogas production provides a useful way of disposing of what would otherwise be a pollutant. Biogas plants in Europe are, however, commercially viable only if supported by subsidies from the European Union because it is cheaper to buy the electricity on the local grid than to generate it from biogas.

Sewage treatment

Sewage is the water-borne waste from toilets, bathrooms, kitchen sinks and washing machines, mixed with some industrial effluents and some natural run-off water from the streets. The main components of sewage are human faeces, urine, paper, bits of food, soap, detergents, household chemicals (like bleach and disinfectants), sand, grit and other road debris, some heavy metals, oils and pesticides. Sewage treatment is the largest biotechnological industry and it is a prime example of the applied use of microorganisms for the control of environmental pollution.

Raw sewage and the environment

If a small quantity of sewage finds its way into a river, aerobic microorganisms of decay (mainly bacteria) perform the useful function of breaking down the organic matter to carbon dioxide and water. The river is thus said to 'clean itself out'. The problem arises when large quantities of raw sewage are discharged into rivers or lakes. The high organic content of the sewage promotes rapid growth of aerobic bacteria of decay, which consume vast quantities of dissolved oxygen. The water soon becomes anaerobic. Fish and other forms of aquatic animal life die from lack of oxygen. Anaerobic bacteria thrive in such conditions, multiplying in great numbers. One type, the sulphate-reducing bacteria, produces hydrogen sulphide gas from sulphates present in the water. The gas has the smell of rotten eggs and it explains why heavily polluted rivers and lakes emit an unpleasant odour.

Untreated sewage has many solid particles suspended in it, which makes the water murky and uninviting. When present in large quantities, the suspended solids reduce light penetration thus restricting photosynthesis and the production of oxygen by submerged water plants and phytoplankton.

Many types of viruses and other pathogenic microorganisms are present in untreated sewage. These microorganisms can cause intestinal diseases, like typhoid, cholera and dysentery, if the contaminated water is consumed.

The treatment of sewage

The main aim in sewage treatment is to remove or reduce the solids and the organic material so that the water can be safely discharged into rivers, lakes or the sea. Sewage treatment can be subdivided into three main phases termed **primary**, **secondary** and **tertiary**.

Primary treatment

The first phase in the treatment of sewage involves the physical means of separating the suspended solids from the waste water. To start with, the incoming sewage is passed through **fixed screens** composed of parallel metal bars placed in the waterways to remove large objects such as rags, sticks, plastic containers, etc. The screens need cleaning regularly by hand or mechanically. The sewage is then directed into **primary sedimentation tanks** where the rate of water flow is considerably reduced to allow grit, sand and other 'settleable solids' to settle to the bottom. The effect is to separate the sewage into solid and aqueous fractions.

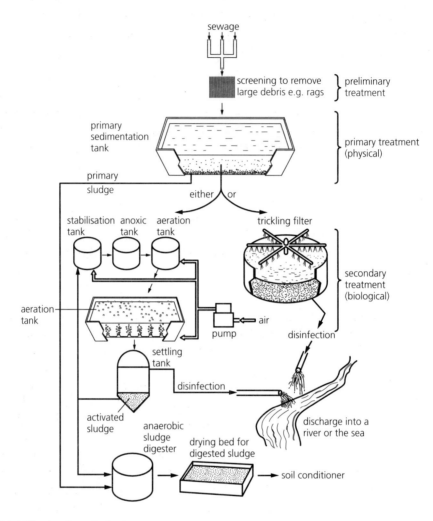

Figure 6.10 The treatment of sewage

Secondary treatment

The aim of this stage is to:

- oxidise the organic matter
- lower the ammonia/nitrate content
- inactivate the pathogenic microorganisms.

Secondary treatment is biological in nature and involves the use of separate procedures for the treatment of the solid and the aqueous fractions after primary treatment.

The solid fraction, which is the material at the bottom of the tank, is called **primary sludge**. It is removed to another tank called an **anaerobic sludge digester**. The supernatant or aqueous fraction, which still contains plenty of organic matter, is subjected to treatment in one of two ways – the **trickling filter system** or the

activated sludge process. The aim in both of these processes is to put the waste water in close contact with as many aerobic bacteria as possible to enable them to feed on the organic matter and to oxidise it to carbon dioxide.

The trickling filter system

In the trickling filter system, the liquid fraction from the settling tanks is sprayed over beds of medium-sized rock chippings in a large, shallow tank, by means of a rotating distributor. The spraying saturates the liquid with air. Various types of microorganisms form a slimy layer over the surface of the chippings. Bacteria are by far the most important, but others include fungi, algae, ciliates and a variety of other protoctists. As the water trickles over the porous material, the organic matter carried in the water is used as food by the microbes and oxidised to carbon dioxide and water by a process of microbial respiration. The carbon dioxide produced escapes into the air. Since the beds are not submerged, oxygen in the air can reach the microbes at all times. About 90% of the soluble organic content of the waste water is removed by this process and the water that trickles through is thus considerably purified.

The activated sludge process

In this process, the aqueous fraction from the settling tanks is directed to an **aeration tank** where the waste water is stirred and vigorously aerated by allowing streams of compressed air to bubble through it via thousands of air diffusers The treatment encourages the growth of aerobic bacteria which feed on the organic matter oxidising it to carbon dioxide and water. Ammonia present in the water is converted to nitrate by aerobic nitrifying bacteria. After 16 hours of aeration, the treated liquid is directed to **final settling tanks** to allow the bacteria, which have multiplied in great numbers, to settle to the bottom leaving the water cleaner. The sludge that settles at the bottom of the tank is teeming with live bacteria and is called **activated sludge**. Most of the activated sludge is removed from the final settling tanks and is returned to the aeration tanks to treat the incoming water. The rest is mixed with the primary sludge (from the primary sedimentation tanks) for treatment by a process of anaerobic digestion. The purified water overflows into channels that discharge into rivers or the sea.

The activated sludge process is highly efficient and is widely used in cities around the world. Up to 98% of the soluble organic content of the waste water is removed by this process. Its main advantages are:

- its efficiency (up to 98% of the soluble organic content of the liquid can be removed)
- the relatively small size of the treatment plant (made possible by the high concentration of active microorganisms in the aeration tank).

Ammonia

Ammonium ions result mainly from the breakdown of urea and other nitrogenous compounds present in the sewage. Given an appropriate pH, ammonium ions can change to ammonia, an alkaline substance that is lethal to fish. **Vigorous bubbling** with air promotes conversion of ammonium ions to nitrates by nitrifying bacteria.

Biological oxygen demand

A useful indicator of water quality is the **biological oxygen demand (BOD)**. The BOD test is done by first measuring the oxygen content of a sample of water. The sealed sample is then maintained at 20 °C for five days and its oxygen content is measured once again. During that time, some of the dissolved oxygen will have been used up by the microorganisms feeding on the organic matter in the water sample. The amount of oxygen used up within the five-day period (abbreviated BOD_5) expressed in milligrams per dm^3 of water is an indirect measure of the organic state of the body of water. In Britain effluents with a BOD_5 less than 25 mg dm^{-3} is considered suitable for discharge into rivers. High-quality water suitable for drinking has a BOD_5 less than 1.5 mg dm^{-3}.

Denitrification

Nitrates in sewage effluents come mainly from fertilisers from suburban lawns. Nitrates can be taken out of the effluents by leading the waste water into an anoxic (oxygen-free) tank to promote the growth of anaerobic denitrifying bacteria.

With a modern sewage works, the denitrification process is usually inserted after the primary sedimentation stage. The supernatant from the primary sedimentation tank is first mixed with 'returned activated sludge' in a stabilisation tank. This tank is strongly aerated to encourage aerobic bacteria in the activated sludge to consume the suspended organic matter in the sewage. The liquid then flows into an anoxic tank, which favours the growth of anaerobic denitrifying bacteria. These bacteria feed on organic matter present in the sewage and respire by stripping oxygen from nitrates, thus converting nitrates into oxides of nitrogen and free molecular oxygen. From the anoxic tank, the mixture is then led to aeration tanks for aerobic treatment as described earlier.

Sludge treatment and disposal

Finally, the solid material or sludge removed from the sedimentation tanks needs to be properly disposed of. The material is 70% organic and still putricible and can be a major pollutant if it is not properly treated before disposal. One method of disposal consists of burning the material in an incinerator but this creates air pollution problems (see box opposite).

In modern sewage treatment plants, the sludge is placed in an airless tank called an **anaerobic sludge digester** to allow anaerobic bacteria including methanogens to feed on the organic material and to degrade it to methane and carbon dioxide. The methane (biogas) is then used to produce electricity for driving the stirrers and the air pumps in the sewage works.

The digested sludge is useful to farmers as a soil conditioner either in liquid form or as a 'compressed cake'. Liquid sludges can be applied to the soil by spraying or injection using special machines. They are also useful as fertilisers because they contain considerable quantities of nitrogen and phosphorus and some potassium. Cake sludge is cheaper to transport but useless as a fertiliser because the soluble mineral content is squeezed out with the liquid.

One highly toxic environmental pollutant linked to waste incineration is a family of chlorinated organic compounds called **dioxins**. Dioxins are by-products of almost all combustion processes. They result from the incomplete burning of chlorinated hydrocarbons. The main sources of dioxins in the environment are incinerators, manufacturers of polyvinyl chloride (PVC) and paper mills.

People exposed to large doses of dioxins develop a disfiguring skin disease known as **chloracne**. Children born to mothers exposed to high levels of dioxins during pregnancy are smaller at birth, less healthy and less intelligent, compared with children whose mothers have not been exposed to high levels of dioxins during pregnancy. Toxicological studies suggest that dioxins bind on to receptors on the nucleus of human and other vertebrate cells, thus mimicking or blocking the action of the mother's sex hormone oestrogen. The effect is to impair development and to slow down growth in the womb. Dioxins have also been linked to the onset of some forms of cancer. A recent report by the US Environmental Protection Agency states that dioxins cause as many as 1 in every 1000 cancers in the US.

Dioxins enter the human food chain from the air, by falling on to grain or pasture that is then eaten by cattle or sheep. They are fat-soluble substances and accumulate in the body fat of animals and in their milk. An analysis of milk fat provides a good indication of dioxin levels in the environment. Background levels of dioxins are between 0.8 and 2.5 picograms (10^{-12} g) per gram of milk fat. Britain's Department of Environment guideline on the daily intake of dioxins in food sets the limit at 1 pg per kg of human body weight. According to a recent study by German scientists, the average daily intake of dioxins in food by adults is 1.3 pg per kg of body weight. On this basis, the assessments of British scientists are that breast-fed babies drink 100 times the recommended limit. The official medical view is that the advantages of breast-feeding still outweigh the danger posed by dioxins in milk. The US Environmental Protection Agency and 13 countries in Europe have recently launched a programme to reduce emissions of chlorine-based chemicals.

Although high temperature incineration worries environmentalists, it is nevertheless the easy way out for the waste disposal industry, which is facing huge increases in the cost of burying industrial and municipal waste. If incinerators are to be used for waste disposal, they should burn the waste at a uniformly high temperature bearing in mind that material at the centre of a burning mass of solid waste may be insulated from the heat and oxygen and may therefore, in reality, be burning at a lower temperature. Incineration at 1200 °C destroys dioxins. The incinerators should also meet strict standards of pollution control and, where appropriate, they should be fitted with catalytic systems designed to destroy dioxins. One type, based on **titanium dioxide**, breaks down dioxins by promoting a reaction between dioxins and oxygen. The catalyst also suppresses chlorine formation and thus prevents dioxins from re-forming in the waste gases.

Toxic effluent processing (tertiary treatment)

Increasingly, treated water is being reused for irrigating crops, cooling nuclear plants and in recreational lakes for boating, fishing and even swimming. Waste water that has undergone biological treatment at the sewage works contains dissolved substances and pathogenic microorganisms. Phosphates, heavy metals, pesticides, enteric viruses and pathogenic bacteria may all be present in toxic concentrations in the biologically treated effluents. If consumed, these substances can affect human health. In the long term, they may also harm aquatic life.

Disinfection

A European Bathing Waters Directive is now in force, which requires holiday resorts to have fewer than 2000 live microbes in 100 millilitres of sea-water. In effect it means that effluents from sewage works near holiday resorts must be disinfected before they are discharged into the sea. One cost-effective method uses **ultraviolet light** to disinfect effluents from sewage works. The treated effluents flow through channels lined by banks of lamps that emit ultraviolet light. The short wavelength light passes through the cell wall and into the microbes disrupting their DNA and thus preventing them from reproducing. As many as 99% of the microbes in treated sewage effluents can be killed using this technique. Chlorine or ozone can also be used to disinfect effluents.

Heavy metals

The main sources of heavy metal contamination in sewage effluents are known. Leather tanneries, for instance, are usually the source of heavy chromium contamination. Cadmium and nickel contamination can usually be traced to factories that make long-life batteries. These and other industries are now required by law to recover metallic ions from industrial effluents before the waste water leaves the factory. This is usually done by **ion exchange**, a process that simply swaps undesirable ions for less troublesome ones.

Some of the nickel, zinc and chromium in sewage effluents results from corrosion of pipes and equipment in homes and factories. This is harder to restrict.

Heavy metals in trace amounts are essential for life. In higher concentrations they can cause growth and metabolic disorders and damage to the nervous system.

Pesticides

Pesticides in sewage effluents come mainly from street run-offs and suburban lawns. Passing the waste water through filter beds of **activated carbon** or pulverised charcoal to which the organic compounds adhere, allows the pesticides to slowly decompose.

Phosphates

Phosphates in sewage effluents are derived mainly from detergents. Unremoved phosphates in sewage effluents can cause environmental pollution problems if the biologically treated water is discharged into streams or lakes. The phosphates promote rapid growth of microscopic algae, a process known as **eutrophication**. Phosphates can be removed by **precipitation** using alum and lime.

Questions

8 Outline the various stages in the treatment of sewage.

9 List the toxic substances that are commonly present in waste water and describe how the concentration of two of them may be lowered before the effluents are discharged into a river.

Degradation of oil spills

Whenever an accident occurs at sea and oil is spilt from a tanker, the oil spreads rapidly to form a slick, which may be many kilometres long. If the oil slick is washed up on a shore line, the beach becomes covered with a thick, black, tarry mat of oily material; this can kill thousands of sea birds, sea mammals and countless other smaller invertebrates.

Hosing with detergents

Attempts to clear the beaches by hosing with detergents are generally never satisfactory. The tide often returns the oil to the seemingly cleaned-up beach and, even worse, the detergents kill natural populations of bacteria that feed on hydrocarbons thus delaying the natural, biological process of recovery of the ecosystem.

Figure 6.11 A victim of an oil spill

Spraying with nitrogen and phosphorus

Laboratory studies show that natural populations of oil-degrading bacteria work only on the oil–water interface. Their growth is also limited by the availability of nutrients, especially nitrogen and phosphorus. One technique for speeding up the biodegradation of an oil spill is to spray **oleophilic (oil-loving) compounds of nitrogen and phosphorus** that will stick to the oil-coated rocks and stones, thus encouraging the growth of the bacteria where they are most required. Another technique consists of spraying the oil slick with a **mixed culture of oil-degrading bacteria** together with appropriate quantities of mineral nutrients.

Genetically engineered oil-consuming 'superbug'

In recent years, biologists have genetically engineered an oil-consuming 'superbug'. The bacterium has been given plasmids carrying genes for degrading different components of oil, such as camphor, naphthalene, xylene, etc. Armed with such an array of oil-degrading enzymes, the genetically engineered bacterium can degrade oil faster than its naturally occurring but less well endowed relatives. The fear, however, is that if such a 'superbug' is released into the natural environment, its DNA may be taken up by other naturally occurring bacteria with unforeseen environmental consequences.

Biodegradable plastics

We live in an age of plastics. Plastics are used to make carrier bags, bottles, boxes, knives and forks, watches, toys, building materials and a whole variety of other household items. Most plastics are derived from petrochemicals. The problem with plastics made from petrochemicals is that, firstly, they are a drain on the world's limited oil reserves and, secondly, they are **non-biodegradable** (i.e. if they are discarded, microorganisms in the soil or water will not break them down). Substances that microorganisms can decompose are said to be **biodegradable**.

Most of the so-called 'biodegradable' carrier bags in use today are only partially biodegradable. They are made from webs of polythene with starch filling the spaces between the webs. The starch decomposes but the remaining constituents resist degradation by microorganisms.

The first truly biodegradable plastic was manufactured by an Italian company called Ferruzzi. The plastic has a 10–50% starch content, the rest consisting of a relatively short-chain, oil-derived molecule that is unusual in that it dissolves in water. This makes the water-soluble substance more amenable to attack by soil and water microorganisms. Ferruzzi's biodegradable plastic, however, costs more to manufacture than the existing plastics.

Biopol

ICI have also developed a truly biodegradable plastic. Manufactured under the trade name Biopol, it is made from a **natural polymer** called polyhydroxybutyrate (PHB). This substance occurs in storage granules in a common bacterium named *Alcaligenes eutrophus*. The bacterium stores PHB granules as an energy reserve in its cytoplasm, in much the same way as humans store fat when food intake exceeds our immediate requirements. It breaks down its stores of PHB when it is deprived of food. Because PHB is a naturally occurring substance, it can readily be degraded by soil and water microorganisms.

Figure 6.12 Biodegradable plastic bottles, made of Biopol by ICI: from left to right **a** new; **b** after 9 weeks; **c** after 35 weeks of aerobic degradation in sewage effluents

To produce PHB, the bacterium is cultured in a bioreactor on a broth of glucose and other essential nutrients. The bacteria feed on the readily available glucose, accumulating PHB in their cytoplasm until as much as 80% of the total bacterial biomass consists of this storage substance. Organic acids, such as propanoic acid, may be added to the nutrient medium used for culturing the bacteria to stimulate production of a series of copolymers, depending on the type of plastic required. The bacteria are then harvested and the polymer is released by rupture of the cells using heat and enzymes. The polymer is then washed and dried to a white powder.

Biopol is more expensive to produce than conventional plastics. It is used to make bottles for a range of biodegradable shampoos. The product was successfully marketed in Germany where public concern for environmental issues is strong. ICI plans to expand its Biopol manufacturing plant to meet increasing demand for its product.

Recovery of metals from mining waste

Microorganisms have also been exploited for use in the mining industry to recover metals from low-grade ores and mining tailings. The metals are dissolved out of the ores by the activities of a type of naturally occurring, rod-shaped, sulphur bacteria called *Thiobacillus ferrooxidans*. These bacteria are **chemoautotrophs**. They feed by synthesising their own organic food molecules from atmospheric carbon dioxide and water, using energy derived from the oxidation of inorganic molecules. They are, in other words, literally 'rock-eaters'. In the course of extracting energy from oxidation of the inorganic material, they bring about the conversion of copper sulphides in the ores to copper sulphate ($CuSO_4$), a soluble mineral.

$$CuS + Fe_2(SO_4)_3 \Rightarrow CuSO_4 + 2FeSO_4 + S$$

Extraction of the metal from low-grade mine waste is normally done on a vast scale. The low-grade ore is transported by road or rail to a dump site, usually a valley with slopes that can hold many millions of tons of the rock-sized material. Water, acidified with sulphuric acid, is sprinkled on top of the dump heap. *T. ferrooxidans* is not inoculated on to the dump heap since it occurs naturally nearly everywhere. The bacteria thrive in moist, acidic conditions and when conditions in the rock pile are suitable, the rock-eating bacteria proliferate and perform their important redox reactions. These reactions result in the conversion of insoluble copper sulphide to soluble copper sulphate. Without the aid of the enzymes that the microorganisms possess, the conversion would occur at much too slow a rate.

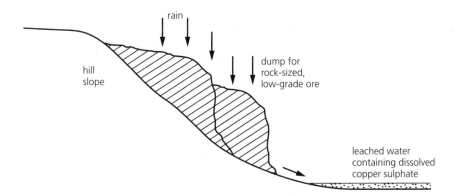

Figure 6.13 Dump leaching – the system uses the bacterium *Thiobacillus ferrooxidans* to extract copper from its low-grade ore

The rusty-brown leach solution that percolates through the rock pile is rich in soluble copper. The percolate collects in basins or reservoirs built at the foot of the rock pile. Elemental copper is later harvested from the copper sulphate solution by running it over scrap iron. The valuable copper precipitates out of the solution as the iron dissolves.

$$CuSO_4 + Fe \Rightarrow Cu + FeSO_4$$

A similar process of bioleaching can be used to extract uranium from its low-grade ore.

Examination questions

1 Silage is cattle feed made from newly cut grass. The grass is allowed to wilt but is not dried before conversion to silage.

    The diagram below shows a silo in which the silage is made and then stored.

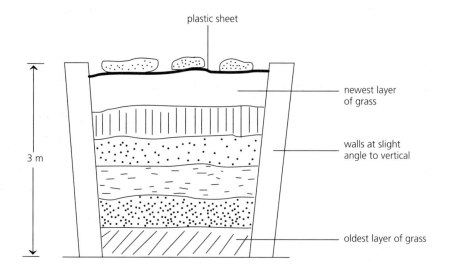

a Describe how microorganisms are involved in the conversion of grass into silage. (3)
b i) Suggest why the grass is allowed to wilt before conversion to silage. (1)
  ii) Suggest why the silage is covered with plastic sheeting. (1)
  iii) Suggest why the silo is constructed with its base narrower than its top. (1)

(total = 6)
ULEAC, June 1996

2 Some bacteria of the genus *Clostridium* are able to perform an anaerobic fermentation of soluble carbohydrates, such as starch or pectin, to produce butanoic acid, ethanoic acid, hydrogen and carbon dioxide.
  a i) Suggest an industrial process or source of waste that might produce a fermentable carbohydrate for these organisms. (1)
  ii) [In the space provided] Draw and label a diagram of a digester where this fermentation could take place. (3)
  iii) Suggest how the digester might be protected from extremes of temperature. (1)
  b i) Suggest **one** use for the hydrogen produced in the digester. (1)
  ii) Outline **one** advantage and **one** disadvantage of this type of fermentation in comparison with a fermentation that produces methane. (4)

(total = 10)
UCLES, June 1995

3 Bacterial samples are tested in a sewage control laboratory. The growth of a particular bacterial culture was followed by taking 1 cm³ samples at regular intervals and then diluting them on nutrient agar plates. The table shows the number of bacterial colonies growing on sample plates taken from the lag phase, the exponential phase and the plateau phase of bacterial growth.

Degrees of dilution (dilution factor)	Number of bacterial colonies per plate		
	Lag phase	Exponential phase	Plateau phase
10^{-4}	55	450	too many to count
10^{-5}	3	37	too many to count
10^{-6}	0	4	195

The number of bacteria in 1 cm³ of the culture is calculated by:

$$\frac{\text{number of colonies per plate} \times 1}{\text{dilution factor}}$$

  a i) Which of the two dilutions (10^{-4} and 10^{-5}) from the lag phase samples is likely to give the most accurate estimate of the concentration of bacteria in the culture at this stage of growth? Explain your answer. (2)
  ii) Estimate the bacterial concentrations in **each** 1 cm³ sample of the three growth phases of the culture. (3)
  b i) State **three** specific constituents of raw sewage that pose a threat to human health. (3)
  ii) State **three** objectives of a sewage management system. (3)
  c Describe the steps involved in an aerobic phase of sewage treatment, indicating the role(s) of microorganisms in the process. (7)
  d What are the reasons for the anaerobic digestion phase of sewage treatment? (2)

(total = 20)
O & C, June 1995

4 Metals such as lead and mercury are very dangerous to humans and also to most microorganisms. There are, however, some microorganisms that can extract metals from their environment. *Thiobacillus ferrooxidans*, for example, has been used to dissolve iron and copper salts from their insoluble ores in the ground.

   a i) Suggest one place where microorganisms that tolerate lead could be found. (1)

     ii) Explain how a pure culture of this microorganism could be obtained. (6)

   b Suggest how the amount of iron and copper that *T. ferrooxidans* could tolerate might be determined. (5)

   c Suggest a reason why some microorganisms are more tolerant of metals such as copper and lead. (1)

(total = 13)

UCLES, June 1995

Suggestions for learning experiences

Activity 4.7. The decomposition of plastic (Investigation) *Advanced Biology Study Guide*, CG Clegg and DG Mackean with PH Openshaw and RC Reynolds. John Murray (Publishers) Ltd 1996, page 57.

Activity 5.1 Visits to a water treatment works (Data generating) *Advanced Biology Study Guide*, CG Clegg and DG Mackean with PH Openshaw and RC Reynolds. John Murray (Publishers) Ltd 1996, page 67.

Activity 5.2 Estimating numbers of microorganisms by the dilution plate method (Skills and techniques) *Advanced Biology Study Guide*, CG Clegg and DG Mackean with PH Openshaw and RC Reynolds. John Murray (Publishers) Ltd 1996, page 69.

Activity 5.4 Biological oxygen demand (Skills and techniques) *Advanced Biology Study Guide*, CG Clegg and DG Mackean with PH Openshaw and RC Reynolds. John Murray (Publishers) Ltd 1996, page 71.

Problem 5.5 Biogas from waste: a design challenge *Advanced Biology Study Guide*, CG Clegg and DG Mackean with PH Openshaw and RC Reynolds. John Murray (Publishers) Ltd 1996, page 81.

Work Card 23 Microbes and water pollution *Practical Microbiology and Biotechnology for Schools*, Paul Wymer. Macdonald Educational 1987.

Enzyme technology

(7)

Enzymes are proteins that function as biological catalysts. After synthesis within the cell, enzymes can function quite independently of the cell, provided certain physical and chemical conditions are maintained. **Enzyme technology** involves the isolation, production and purification of enzymes, and their use in service industries; it aims to produce substances of commercial value.

Commercial enzymes are obtained from three main sources – plant, animal and microorganisms. In the manufacture of beer, for example, the starch-digesting enzyme amylase is obtained from germinating barley seeds. Papain, a proteolytic plant enzyme used in meat tenderisation, is extracted from the latex of the papaya plant. In the manufacture of cheese, the rennet used for curdling milk is traditionally extracted from the stomachs of unweaned calves. Apart from these, most industrial enzymes are of microbial origin and are produced by a process of **submerged fermentation** using liquid culture media. There are some industrial fungal enzymes that are produced using semi-solid culture media.

Enzyme production by submerged fermentation

Most bacterial and some fungal enzymes are produced industrially by batch culture of specially selected strains of microorganisms using liquid media. Large, stainless-steel tanks between 100 and 200 m³ are used for culturing the microorganisms. The source of carbon for the culture is usually a cheap, easily available substrate such as corn steep liquor, molasses, starch hydrolysate or whey. Ammonium salts, urea or peptones are usually chosen to provide a source of nitrogen. Various minerals, vital trace elements and vitamins may also be supplied to meet the nutritional needs of the particular microorganism.

Sterilisation is achieved by the use of steam at 121 °C for 30–60 minutes. When the sterilised nutrient medium has cooled to the propagation temperature and the medium has been adjusted to its optimum pH, aseptic procedures are used to introduce the inoculum into the production tank. Since the chosen microorganism is nearly always aerobic, compressed air (sterilised by filtration through glass wool or activated carbon) is bubbled through the liquid medium via a sparger at the base of the tank. Several impellers are usually provided for mixing the contents of the bioreactor. The temperature within the bioreactor is controlled by circulating water through a jacket or coil that surrounds the tank. As the fermentation process gets under way, refrigerated water is usually circulated to remove the heat produced by microbial respiration. The temperature within the bioreactor is continuously monitored using a temperature probe and the information is fed to a computer that automatically sets in motion the necessary adjustments for maintaining the temperature at an optimum level (usually between 25 and 37 °C). Auxiliary tanks are provided for adding nutrients, acids or alkalis (for maintaining optimum pH) and antifoaming agents, such as lard oil or silicone compounds.

The growth of the culture is regularly monitored, and changes in broth composition, pH and temperature are continually checked and corrections made where appropriate. The time for microbial propagation and enzyme production can be anything from 18 hours to seven days depending on the microbial species. During this period, every precaution is taken to exclude contaminants and to maintain a pure culture.

Extraction of the enzyme

If the desired enzyme is secreted extracellularly, it will be present dissolved in the spent fermentation liquor. The first step in the extraction of the enzyme would then be the separation of the solution from the cells and the insoluble substances. This is achieved by centrifugation or filtration, usually with the aid of flocculants.

Intracellular enzymes are retained within the cells. The first step in the extraction of an intracellular enzyme is the separation of the cells from the spent broth. The cells are then disrupted, usually by mechanical methods or by ultrasound, and the cell sap is separated from the insoluble residue by centrifugation or filtration. The residue is washed to recover more of the enzyme using water buffered to the optimum pH for maintaining enzyme stability.

The next step consists of concentrating the enzyme solution by removal of the bulk of its water content. This is achieved by low-temperature vacuum evaporation, reverse osmosis or a combination of these techniques. In reverse osmosis, a very high pressure is used to force the water out through a partially permeable membrane, thus leaving the enzyme solution more concentrated. Preservatives are then added and the syrupy product may be packaged as such for distribution to industrial users. Most low-priced industrial enzymes are crude products consisting of a mixture of proteinaceous substances.

Where enzymes are required in powder form, the semi-crude solution containing the enzyme is mixed with inert substances and then shaped by spray drying or by drying on trays. If pure enzymes are required, techniques such as fractional precipitation, crystallisation or adsorption may be employed.

Enzyme immobilisation

The widespread use of industrial enzymes has brought with it a problem: how to recover for re-use expensive enzymes that, at the end of the reaction, are found mixed with the product within the spent substrate. The answer to this came with a recent development known as **enzyme immobilisation**. It involves the conversion of a water-soluble enzyme into a water-insoluble product that still possesses the specific catalytic activity of the enzyme.

The immobilisation of an enzyme (or cell) can be achieved in four main ways (see also Figure 7.1):

1 adsorption
2 covalent attachment
3 entrapment within polymer gels
4 direct cross-linking.

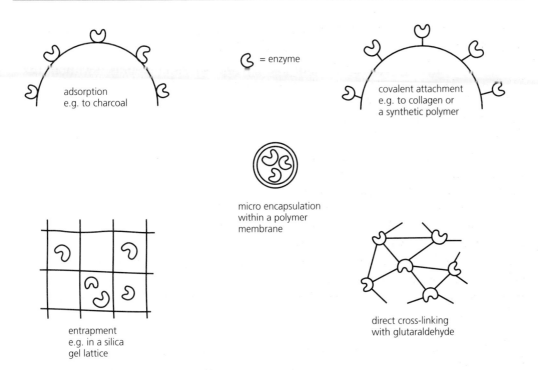

Figure 7.1 Methods of enzyme immobilisation

Adsorption

Being proteins, enzymes have many positively or negatively charged amino acid side-chains on their surface. These charges are attracted to weak electrostatic forces on the surface of insoluble substances (such as ion-exchange resins, alumina or clay), thus enabling the enzyme to adhere to the solid support. One disadvantage of this technique is that the enzyme molecules eventually wash away; although, surprisingly long useful 'lives' have been reported. Another disadvantage is that the charges on the solid support may cause local pH disturbances around the microenvironment of the enzyme, thus affecting its rate of activity.

Covalent attachment

This technique requires the use of reagents that can cause the enzyme to react covalently with the surface of a solid support, for example collagen or some synthetic polymer. The covalent bonding must not, of course, involve the parts of the enzyme needed for enzyme activity. It is the preferred technique because covalent attachments are stable. However, it is difficult to immobilise enzymes in this way.

Entrapment within polymer gels

When an enzyme is mixed with certain 'polymerisable' substances such as vinyl monomers, the meshwork of fibres that form during polymerisation yields a gel with enzyme molecules trapped in the spaces between the fibres. A disadvantage of this technique is that both the substrate molecules and the reaction products must be small enough to diffuse freely in and out of the gelatinous matrix.

Direct cross-linking

Glutaraldehyde is used to cross-link the enzyme molecules to one another. The polymerised enzyme precipitates out of solution and is thus immobilised without the use of a solid support.

Advantages of using immobilised enzymes

- Easy recovery of the enzyme for re-use over and over again. This is especially important when the enzyme is expensive.
- Easy harvesting of the reaction products free from contamination by the enzyme.
- Greater enzyme stability due to protection offered by the inert matrix.
- Ideally suited for use in continuous fermentation processes.
- Extends the useful 'life' of proteolytic enzymes by preventing the enzyme molecules from digesting one another.

Some loss of enzymatic activity

One disadvantage of enzyme immobilisation is that the attachment to a solid support often results in some loss of enzymatic activity. This may arise because:

- the attachment occurs too near the active site of the enzyme
- the chemical reaction denatures the active site
- the transport of the reactants is hindered by the unstirred layer of molecules surrounding the immobilised enzyme particle.

Advantages of using cell-free enzymes compared with whole cells

Many traditional industrial processes still use whole living cells as catalysts. However, with the development of immobilised enzymes, there is an increasing demand for purified cell-free enzymes. The advantages of using cell-free enzymes compared with the use of whole cells are:

- when whole cells are used, a substantial proportion of the substrate is converted into microbial biomass, whereas with cell-free enzymes the substrate is not wasted in this way
- the optimal conditions for the culture of whole cells may not be optimal for product formation
- there are no wasteful side-reactions when purified cell-free enzymes are used
- the procedure for harvesting and isolating the product is simpler if only a single product is made.

Whole cells are advantageous when the enzyme is expensive or difficult to extract or when the process involves a chain of interconnected reactions.

Questions

1 Describe how industrial enzymes are produced.
2 What are immobilised enzymes?
3 What are the advantages of using enzymes compared with inorganic catalysts in manufacturing industries?

Uses of industrial enzymes

Industrial enzymes are used in almost every field where organic substances of plant or animal origin are processed into consumer goods. They are used in the manufacture of bread, biscuits, dairy products, confectionery, fruit juices, flavourings, beer, wines, carbonated drinks, distilled beverages, biological detergents and pharmaceuticals.

The manufacture of high-fructose corn syrups

Corn starch is a cheap, readily available carbohydrate. It is the starting point for the manufacture of high-fructose corn syrups, a product used as a sweetener in the manufacture of canned soft drinks.

   The starch is first heat-treated to cause it to gelatinise. Two microbial enzymes, α amylase and amyloglucosidase, are then used to degrade the starch to glucose. Glucose is not a particularly sweet sugar; its isomer fructose, however, is much sweeter. Another microbial enzyme, **glucose isomerase**, is used to convert glucose to fructose.

Immobilisation of glucose isomerase

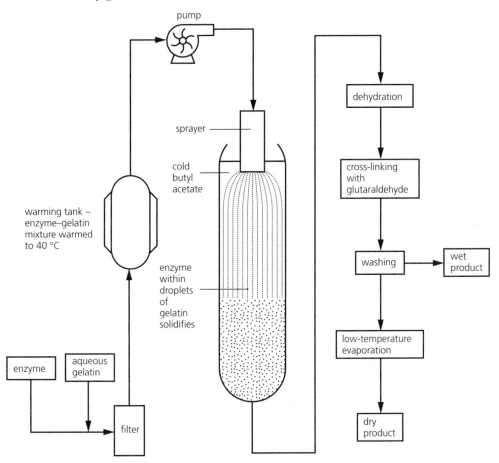

Figure 7.2 A flow diagram for the immobilisation of glucose isomerase

Glucose isomerase is produced intracellularly and is consequently an expensive enzyme. To immobilise glucose isomerase, the crude enzyme preparation is mixed with an aqueous solution of gelatin, followed by warming to 40 °C. The mixture is then sprayed into a column containing a cold, immiscible solvent such as butyl acetate. The effect is to cause droplets of gelatin containing the enzyme to solidify and settle to the bottom of the column. The particles are then partially dehydrated in alcohol and cross-linked by treatment with glutaraldehyde. The immobilised enzyme particles are then washed and packed into a tall column.

Continuous isomeration of glucose

Glucose syrup is pumped into the top of the column and, as it flows down, the glucose molecules are converted by the immobilised enzyme into fructose. This process of continuous isomeration is highly cost effective. The desired product is harvested from the bottom, free from contamination by the enzyme, which remains active for up to 100 days. Millions of tonnes of fructose are produced annually by this method.

The production of lactose-free milk

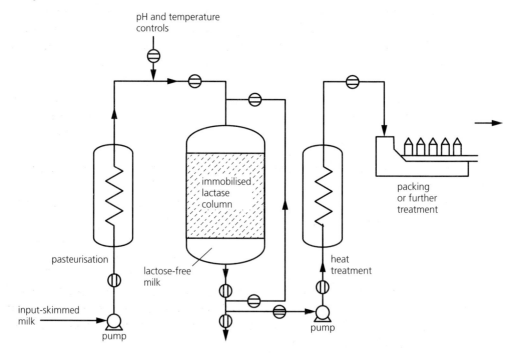

Figure 7.3 The continuous production of lactose-free milk

Milk is an important item in the human diet. It contains the disaccharide sugar lactose, which is broken down in the small intestine to glucose and galactose by an enzyme called lactase. There are, however, many adult humans especially in the Far East and around the Mediterranean who are deficient in this enzyme and are said to be **lactose intolerant**. They suffer abdominal distension, severe abdominal pains, flatulence and acid diarrhoea if they consume even a small quantity of milk. The problem is that the lactose passes through their small intestine undigested and, on reaching the colon, is fed upon by colon bacteria. These bacteria release (as products of lactose fermentation) fatty acids, especially ethanoic and butanoic acids, and the gases methane, carbon dioxide and hydrogen. It is the production of these gases and acids which is responsible for the symptoms of discomfort experienced by lactose intolerant individuals.

To make milk acceptable to lactose-intolerant people, the lactose needs to be taken out of the milk. Lactose-free milk is made by passing heat-sterilised skimmed milk down a reaction column packed with **immobilised lactase**. The lactose-free milk that emerges at the bottom of the column is then packaged for sale to consumers. The process is, however, prone to infection as it occurs at neutral pH and at moderately low temperatures.

The clarification of fruit juices

Fruit juices, such as apple juice, contain **pectins**. These are a group of complex carbohydrates that bind neighbouring plant cells together; they occur in the middle lamella between plant cells. In the presence of divalent ions, such as calcium ions, pectins form gels that set like jam, thus causing viscosity problems for the fruit juice manufacturer. Pectins can also form colloids with proteins, and this is responsible for haze formation and also gives rise to filtration problems for the fruit juice manufacturer.

Immobilised pectinase is now widely used to overcome these problems. Pectinase consists of a mixture of different pectin-degrading enzymes. The fruit juice is passed through a column packed with the immobilised enzymes. Some of the enzymes act by coagulating colloidal pectin; others degrade it into short-chain oligosaccharides.

Microbial cellulases and **hemicellulases** are also used for fruit juice manufacture. These enzymes act by degrading the principal components of the cell wall, thus accelerating the extraction of the fruit juices and the liquefaction and extraction of colour pigments from the skin and peel of some types of fruits.

Meat tenderisation

Bacteria, fungi and many plants, including papaya, pineapple and fig, produce non-toxic proteolytic enzymes capable of hydrolysing meat proteins. When used as a meat tenderiser, the enzyme attacks the connective tissue that binds muscle fibres together as well as the muscle fibres themselves.

Muscle tissue contains its own proteolytic enzymes (packaged within membrane-enveloped organelles called lysosomes). When meat is hung, these proteolytic enzymes gradually break down the muscle structure. This is why traditional butchers speak fondly of 'well hung beef' because they know that, after two or three weeks of hanging, the meat will be deliciously tender. The use of proteolytic enzymes as meat tenderisers cuts out the need for hanging. Meat tenderised and slaughtered one day can be eaten the next day, thus saving on storage costs.

The difficulty with the use of meat tenderisers is that if the tenderising solution is injected into the joint after slaughter, the meat tends to react to the enzyme in patches leaving the meat mushy at some places and tough at others. Dipping in the tenderiser is also unsatisfactory because the meat becomes mushy and over-tenderised at the surface. The most effective method consists of injection into the jugular vein up to half an hour before slaughter. The technique makes use of the animal's own blood stream to distribute the tenderiser. Excess enzyme is drained off after slaughter when the carcass is bled. Advocates of this technique claim that the injected enzyme does no harm to the live animal. Animal welfare groups, however, have voiced their objection on the grounds that the technique is an unnecessary interference and there is also no way of knowing whether it actually causes suffering.

Biological detergents

Large quantities of industrial enzymes are needed for the manufacture of biological washing powders and liquids. Most of the enzymes used in detergents are produced by **thermophilic bacteria**. These are heat-loving bacteria that normally live in environments, such as hot springs, where the ambient temperature is above 45 °C. Thermophilic bacteria can also be found in large numbers within large compost heaps where the temperature is often above 65 °C.

There are definite advantages in using the enzymes of thermophiles in biological washing powders and liquids: firstly, compared with the enzymes of mesophiles (organisms that live in more moderate ambient conditions, that is, between 18 and 45 °C), those of thermophiles are more stable and enjoy longer shelf-lives under normal laundry conditions; secondly, stains are easier to dislodge at higher temperatures.

A range of microbial enzymes are commonly incorporated into biological washing powders and liquids, including proteases, amylases and cellulases. Protein stains like blood, egg, and milk are difficult to remove by detergent action alone because they are insoluble in water and cling tightly to the fabric.

Proteases in biological detergents act by degrading proteins to oligopeptides, thus making the stain water-soluble or at least water-permeable. This allows the detergents in the washing powders to act on the stain and to disperse it into the water.

Machine dishwasher detergents contain **bacterial α-amylase** to remove starch stains. Fat stains, such as cooking fat, are more difficult to remove. There are technological problems associated with the use of fat-digesting enzymes.

A recent development is the addition of **cellulases** into biological washing powders and liquids. The cellulases degrade cellulose microfibrils that form on cotton fibres during washing and wearing, leaving the fabric feeling smoother and looking brighter in colour.

Questions

4 Name three industrial enzymes and describe their roles in the laundry industry.
5 Outline the main steps in the production of lactose-free milk.
6 Describe the role of enzymes in the manufacture of fruit juices.

A summary of the industrial uses of enzymes

Enzyme	Industry	Primary action on substrate	Purpose
bacterial α-amylase	beverage	hydrolyses starch in fruit juice	prevents haze formation
	automatic dishwashing	liquefies starch residues	manufacture of automatic dishwashing powders
fungal α-amylase	baking	hydrolyses starch flour to maltose	yeast cannot degrade starch but can break down maltose to ethanol and carbon dioxide
microbial cellulase	laundry	degrades cellulose microfibrils	colour brightener
	beverage	hydrolyses cellulose to glucose	degrades plant cell walls thus accelerating fruit juice extraction and the extraction of colour from certain fruits
yeast lactase	dairy	hydrolyses lactose to glucose and galactose	production of lactose-free milk
			manufacture of ice-cream
fungal lipase	dairy	hydrolyses fats	enhances the flavour of cheese during ripening
	cleaning	hydrolyses fats	manufacture of grease-trap digesters and drain cleaner formulations
microbial pectinase	beverage	hydrolyses pectins	lowers the viscosity of the extracted fruit juice, improves filtration and prevents haze formation
	food processing	hydrolyses pectins	extraction of colour from fruit peel
fungal acid protease	dairy	coagulates the milk protein casein	replacement for calf rennet in the manufacture of cheese
bacterial protease	baking	lowers the protein content of flour	manufacture of biscuits
bacterial alkaline protease	laundry and cleaning	degrades protein stains such as milk, egg and blood to oligopeptides	manufacture of biological detergents

Examination questions

1 Enzymes are used industrially in a wide range of applications. The majority of these enzymes are extracted from microorganisms such as bacteria and yeasts.

The diagram below represents the stages involved in the production of an isolated enzyme.

Cells → Disruption of cells → Removal of debris → Purification → Isolated enzyme

a i) Suggest *two* advantages of using microorganisms as a source of enzymes.(2)
ii) Suggest *two* advantages of using isolated enzymes rather than whole organisms in industrial processes. (2)
iii) Suggest *one* disadvantage of using isolated enzymes in industrial processes. (1)
b Purified enzymes are frequently immobilised. This means that the enzyme molecules are attached to an insoluble support or trapped within spheres of gel. One simple method of immobilising an enzyme in the laboratory is to mix it with a solution of sodium alginate and then, using a syringe, allow drops of the mixture to fall into a solution of calcium chloride. The alginate/enzyme mixture forms beads, which are allowed to stand in the calcium chloride solution for 20 minutes to become firm. They are then strained from the calcium chloride solution, rinsed and packed into a column ready for use. The enzyme substrate can be added to the column and the products can be collected at the bottom. These events are summarised in the diagram below.

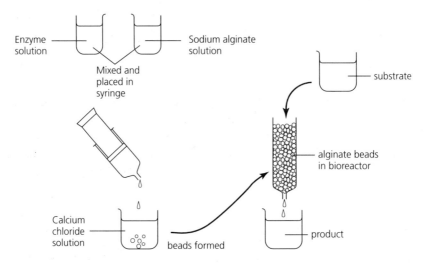

i) State *two* factors which would affect the rate at which the products would be formed in such a system. (2)
ii) Suggest *two* advantages of using immobilised enzymes rather than enzymes in solution. (2)
c Name *two* enzymes used in the food industry and in each case briefly describe its application. (6)   (total = 15)

ULEAC, June 1994

2 Enzymes are commonly used in the food industry and are also found as constituents of biological detergents.
a Suggest four reasons why it is advantageous to use enzymes in the food industry. (4)
b In the first biological detergents to be marketed, the instructions stated that for the best results soiled clothing should be soaked in the detergent in warm water for a period of time prior to washing in hot water. Give a biological explanation for this. (2)
c In some modern dishwashing powders there are at least three different enzymes. Suggest why this is so. (2)   (total = 8)

UODLE, June 1995

3 Read the following passage.

Starch is the main storage carbohydrate in most higher plants and is found as insoluble granules in the cytoplasm. It is a mixture of two glucose polymers; amylopectin, a branched polysaccharide that makes up 75–85% of most starches, and amylose, a linear polysaccharide.

Corn starch is a very cheap chemical feedstock and may be converted to fructose using various microbial enzymes. A starch suspension is heated to 105 °C and the granules swell to form a thick paste. α-amylase obtained from bacteria is added to the viscous paste at this stage. It is a very thermo-stable enzyme and it begins to hydrolyse the starch and reduce the viscosity of the paste. The temperature is then lowered to 90 °C and hydrolysis continues for 1–2 hours. α-amylase is an endoenzyme that hydrolyses bonds within the polysaccharide molecule so that long chains are broken into smaller branched units called dextrins.

The next step involves the conversion of dextrins to glucose and is carried out by a fungal enzyme, amyloglucosidase. The substrate is adjusted to conditions producing the maximum rate of reaction, a temperature of 60 °C and a pH of 4.5, before the enzyme is added. Amyloglucosidase is an exoenzyme, removing glucose a molecule at a time, from one end of the dextrin molecule.

The resulting glucose syrup, after concentration, can be converted into fructose. This process involves glucose isomerase produced by bacteria. Glucose isomerase is an intracellular enzyme bound to cell membranes and is expensive to extract and use as a soluble reagent. It is therefore normally immobilised by binding it to cellulose particles.

Using information in the passage and your own knowledge, answer the following questions.

a Draw a simple flow chart showing the chemical steps in the conversion of starch to fructose. Indicate on your flow chart the enzymes that control these steps. (2)

b i) Using information contained in the passage and giving reasons for your answer, identify the carbohydrate whose chemical structure is shown below:
  ii) Show how the part of the molecule shown in the box is hydrolysed. (2)
c What is meant by a thermo-stable enzyme? (1)
d Explain why the viscosity of the paste is reduced. (1)
e i) What is the difference between the action of an endoenzyme and that of an exoenzyme? (2)
  ii) Suggest why it is more effective to add an endoenzyme before using an exoenzyme in the hydrolysis of a large molecule like starch. (2)

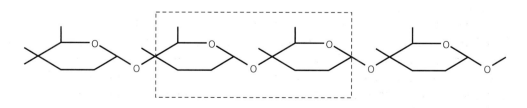

  f Sketch graphs to show the likely effect of the following on the activity of amyloglucosidase:
    i) variation in temperature (2)
    ii) variation in pH. (2)
  g Explain the advantage of using glucose isomerase as an immobilised enzyme rather than free in solution. (3)   (total = 20)

AEB (Specimen Paper), 1996

Suggestions for learning experiences

Activity 5.5 Industrial uses of enzymes: fruit juice production (Investigation) *Advanced Biology Study Guide*, CG Clegg and DG Mackean with PH Openshaw and RC Reynolds. John Murray (Publishers) Ltd 1996, page 72.

Activity 5.8 An introduction to immobilised enzymes (Investigation) *Advanced Biology Study Guide*, CG Clegg and DG Mackean with PH Openshaw and RC Reynolds. John Murray (Publishers) Ltd 1996, page 76.

Problem 5.7 Testing for enzymes in 'biological' washing powder *Advanced Biology Study Guide*, CG Clegg and DG Mackean with PH Openshaw and RC Reynolds. John Murray (Publishers) Ltd 1996, page 81.

Enzyme Isolation: Investigations in Applied Biology and Biotechnology, Peter Freeland. Hodder & Stoughton 1990, page 5.

8

Biotechnology in medicine, health care and forensic science

Arguably, the greatest impact of biotechnology has been in the fields of medicine and health care. We have already seen how millions of people with diabetes have been helped by human insulin produced cheaply by genetically engineered bacteria. There are recent reports that the deadly human disease AIDS is showing signs of yielding to a combination of new drugs made available by biotechnology. A diagnostic technique has recently been developed to detect bladder cancer through the presence of unusual proteins in the urine. The significance of this new development is that we will now be able to spot the cancer at an early stage and thus considerably increase the chances of successful treatment against the ailment. Sufferers of cystic fibrosis can look forward to the day when they would no longer need to endure daily treatment to clear the sticky mucus from their lungs, now that, through biotechnology, the underlying genetic defect has been pinpointed. These are just a few of the medical and health-care benefits that humankind has reaped from advances in biotechnology.

Monoclonal antibodies

One product of biotechnology that has both medical as well as other uses is **monoclonal antibodies**. All vertebrates, including humans, produce antibodies to react with and to mark out for destruction foreign substances such as viruses, bacteria or alien proteins (collectively known as **antigens**). Human antibodies are produced by certain white blood cells of the immune system called **B-lymphocytes**. Each individual possesses millions of different lines of B-lymphocytes. Each type is genetically programmed to produce just one type of antibody. When an antigen enters the body it eventually encounters a B-lymphocyte displaying a matching antibody. Binding of the antigen to the antibody activates the B-lymphocyte, triggering a series of profound changes in the cell. It swells and actively divides, giving rise to a clone of daughter cells. Some of the daughter cells enlarge to become antibody-secreting **plasma cells**. Each plasma cell is capable of secreting more than 10 million copies of a particular type of antibody molecule per hour.

Fusing two types of cells to produce hybridomas

Attempts have been made to culture plasma cells individually as a way of obtaining a large supply of a specific antibody. However, plasma cells are highly specialised cells and they will not divide in culture. They are consequently rather short-lived and do not stay alive long enough to make the effort worthwhile. This difficulty was eventually solved in 1975 by using a **fusing agent** (ethane-1,2-diol) to cause fusion of antibody-secreting lymphocytes (extracted from the spleen of a mouse) with mouse **myeloma (tumour) cells**. The latter are cancerous cells that will actively divide in a culture solution but the antibodies they produce are abnormal. The product of cell fusion between a plasma cell and a myeloma cell is called a **hybridoma**. Hybridoma cells divide actively and produce antibodies continuously. They can therefore be cloned. Since each clone of hybridoma cells produces just one type of antibody, the antibodies they produce are known as **monoclonal antibodies**.

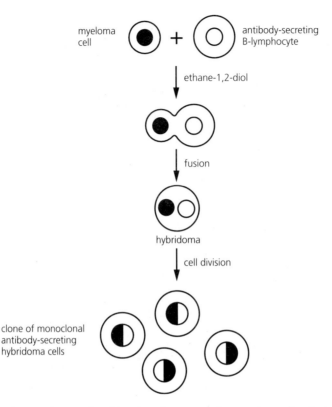

Figure 8.1 Fusing myeloma cells with B-lymphocytes to form a clone of actively dividing, antibody-secreting hybridoma cells

Large-scale production

The large-scale production of monoclonal antibodies can be subdivided into seven steps.

1 **Immunisation** – A mouse is injected with a purified antigen (or a mixture of antigens) to stimulate antibody production by its immune system against the chosen antigen.

2 **Splenectomy** – Antibody-secreting plasma cells are then extracted from the spleen of the mouse.

3 **Fusion** – The plasma cells are fused in the presence of ethane-1,2-diol with mouse myeloma cells deficient in an enzyme called HPGRT (hypoxanthine-guanine-phosphoribosyltransferase).

4 **Cloning** – The fused cells are divided into individual cultures by dilution and incubated in a medium containing a substance called HAT (hypoxanthine-aminopterin-thymidine). Only cells that have successfully been fused will grow and multiply in this culture medium.

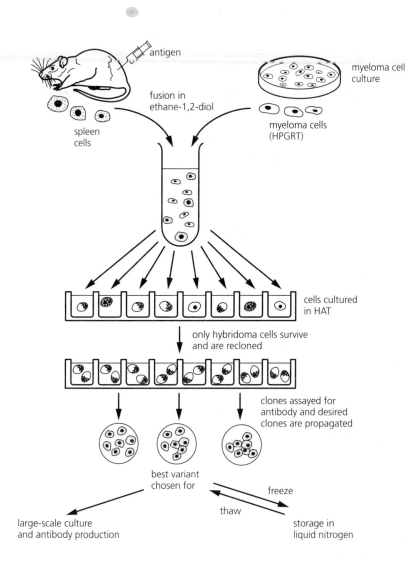

Figure 8.2 The procedure for monoclonal antibody production

5 **Selection** – Two to four weeks later, a small sample of the culture medium from each culture is tested for the presence of the desired specific antibodies. If they are found to be present, the cells from that culture are selected for large-scale culture.

6 **Large-scale culture** – Unlike microorganisms that are encased in a tough cell wall, mammalian cells are fragile and their nutritional requirements are more stringent. Shear forces can rupture them rather easily. The large-scale culture is, therefore, done in an airlift fermenter that works without impellers.

7 **Extraction and purification** – Since the monoclonal antibodies are secreted into the medium, the desired product is first separated from the cells by filtration and is then concentrated and purified.

Uses of monoclonal antibodies

Monoclonal antibodies are used in a variety of ways.

Treatment of certain diseases

Monoclonal antibodies can be used to treat diseases such as rabies or tetanus, where it would be too late to take other therapeutic measures. Mouse antibodies, however, cannot be given in large quantities to humans as the body's immune system soon recognises them as foreign and clears them away.

Making drugs for blocking organ transplant rejection

Monoclonal antibodies have recently been used for making drugs designed to prevent organ transplant rejection by the body's immune system. The drug is injected into the organ through the artery before transplantation. The monoclonal antibodies in the drug act by neutralising mature white blood cells that would otherwise attack the new organ.

The purification of proteins

Monoclonal antibodies can be coupled to certain resins and used to purify a desired protein, for example interferon. To do this, monoclonal antibodies that bind to interferon molecules are immobilised by attaching them to an insoluble substance, such as a synthetic polymer resin. The beads of resin with the monoclonal antibodies attached to their surfaces are then packed into a column. A crude preparation of interferon, extracted from a culture of genetically engineered bacteria, is then poured down the column. As the mixture of proteins trickles down the column, the interferon molecules bind on to the immobilised antibodies and are thus retained by the beads. All other proteins pass through to the bottom of the column. A weak acid is then poured down the column. The acid dislodges the interferon. The solution containing the interferon is then neutralised and concentrated by low-temperature evaporation or reverse osmosis.

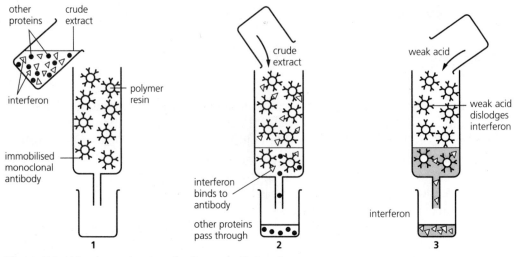

Figure 8.3 Using monoclonal antibodies to purify interferon

The pregnancy test

The pregnancy test works by making use of monoclonal antibodies to detect the presence of the pregnancy hormone, **human chorionic gonadotropin (HCG)** in urine. The hormone is secreted by the placenta. In a pregnancy test, a few drops of urine are placed at the base of a test slide, which has been pre-coated with an absorbent substance. At the basal end of the test slide, the absorbent material is impregnated with coloured, mobile monoclonal antibodies against HCG. If HCG molecules are present in the urine, they will bind specifically to the mobile antibodies and the HCG–antibody complexes travel by capillary action up the slide with the urine.

About halfway up the slide, the HCG–antibody complexes are stopped by a row of immobilised monoclonal antibodies that also bind HCG. Accumulation of HCG–antibody complexes at this level produces a blue line across the slide, indicating that that the woman is pregnant. Coloured, mobile antibodies that are not bound to HCG molecules will continue travelling further up the slide to be stopped by another row of immobilised antibodies that bind specifically to them. Thus, if HCG is present in the urine sample, a blue line will appear in **both** the large window half way up the slide as well as in the small window further up the slide. The test is negative if a blue line appears only in the small window of the slide.

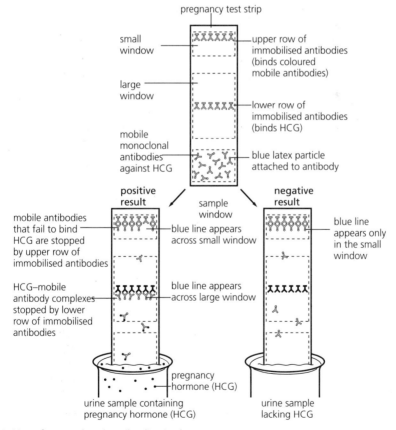

Figure 8.4 Use of monoclonal antibodies in the pregnancy test

Questions

1 What are monoclonal antibodies?
2 Outline the main steps in the production of monoclonal antibodies.
3 Explain how monoclonal antibodies are used in the purification of proteins.
4 Explain how the pregnancy test works.

Biosensors

Another product of biotechnology with medical and health-care uses is the
biosensor. Biosensors are electronic monitoring devices that use biological material
to detect substances in the environment. One such device is an **enzyme-coated
biochip** used to detect and measure the concentration of glucose in the blood. It has
as its key component the enzyme **glucose oxidase**, which is immobilised on to the
surface of a semiconducting silicon chip. The enzyme catalyses the conversion of
glucose to gluconic acid.

$$\text{glucose} + O_2 + H_2O \Rightarrow \text{gluconic acid} + H_2O_2$$

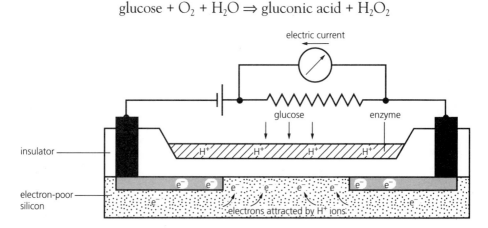

Figure 8.5 A glucose biosensor – made in the form of a biochip. It consists of an acid-producing
enzyme immobilised on to a semiconducting silicon chip

When glucose comes into contact with the enzyme, the H^+ ions of the gluconic acid
give a positive charge to the upper surface of the insulating material between the
enzyme and the chip. This has the effect of attracting electrons around the silicon
terminals, thus causing an electric current to flow. The size of the current is
proportional to the concentration of glucose in the blood. Biosensors of this type are
used by people with diabetes for measuring blood sugar levels.

Nationwide health screening using a multiple biosensor

Researchers in Japan have recently invented a **multiple biosensor cartridge**, for use in specially designed toilets, that can simultaneously measure the levels of glucose, lactate, uric acid, urea and antibodies in urine. Each biosensor is used once. After use, it slides aside to present a fresh biosensor. The device will initially be used in toilets in geriatric day centres to monitor the health of old people but has the potential for widespread use for nationwide health screening. The information from the biosensors is fed to a computer and modem, which would then flag up warning signals to a doctor's office. Glucose levels are for diagnosing diabetes. Lactate levels are an indicator of stress and fatigue. Uric acid and urea are indicators of kidney malfunction, and antibody levels are useful indicators of infectious diseases and cancer.

DNA fingerprinting or profiling

One product of medical research that proved to be very useful for police and forensic work is **DNA profiling** or **fingerprinting**. It is a way of making a pattern from pieces of DNA (cut with restriction enzymes) that is unique to every individual. To understand the DNA fingerprinting method, it is necessary to review briefly the structure of the DNA molecule.

DNA is a long-chain, double-helical molecule composed of building units called **nucleotides**. Each nucleotide consists of a sugar phosphate attached to a nitrogenous base. There are four types of nitrogenous bases – adenine, guanine, cytosine and thymine. The genetic information carried by a DNA molecule is contained in the sequence of these four bases. A gene is a length of DNA that contains the information for specifying a polypeptide. In human cells, the DNA molecules are organised into chromosomes located within the nucleus. Each human chromosome contains about 4000 genes. Surprisingly, only 2% of the total DNA of a human cell consists of genes. The rest consists of non-coding sequences of DNA called **introns**. Each intron can be between 60 and 100 000 nucleotides long. A single gene can harbour as many as 50 of these introns sandwiched between **exons**, which are the coding parts of the DNA molecule. The function of these non-coding introns is unknown.

Minisatellites or VNTRs

Within certain major introns there are short sequences of bases that repeat themselves over and over again, sometimes up to 100 times. These repeating regions of DNA are called **minisatellites** or **VNTRs** (variable number tandem repeats). The greater the number of repeats, the longer the minisatellite.

DNA fingerprinting is based on two important observations. Firstly, the number of repeats tends to vary considerably from person to person; secondly, each individual has 50–100 different types of minisatellites. The trick in DNA profiling is to focus on the most variable or **polymorphic** minisatellites. The chances of any two individuals having matching VNTRs, all of the same length, is likely to be minuscule (unless, of course, the two are identical twins).

Making a DNA fingerprint

The technique for making a DNA fingerprint or profile can be subdivided into four main steps. These are:

1 extraction   2 digestion   3 separation   4 hybridisation.

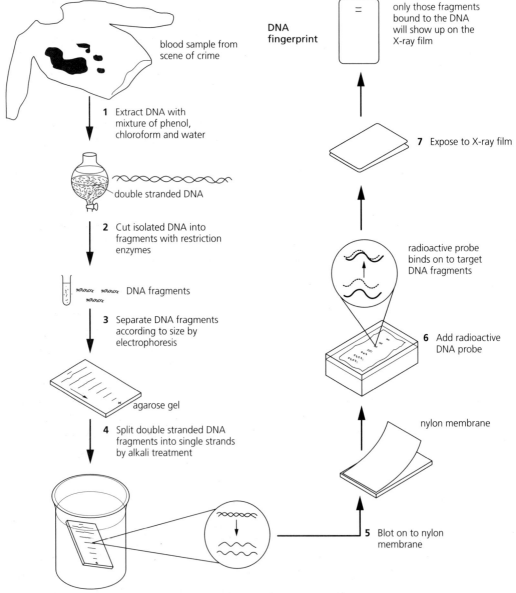

Figure 8.6 DNA fingerprinting

Extraction

A sample of tissue-containing cells (e.g. a drop of blood, a hair root, a few sperm cells, etc.) is recovered and taken to a laboratory where the DNA is extracted by shaking the sample in a mixture of water-saturated phenol and chloroform. The proteins precipitate out, leaving pure DNA dissolved in the water layer.

Digestion

Certain restriction enzymes are then added to cut the DNA at particular points into a number of fragments, each large enough to contain non-coding regions.

Separation

The DNA fragments are then separated according to size by **electrophoresis**. This involves placing the DNA fragments in wells at one end of a slab of agarose gel (extracted from kelp, a sea weed). An electric current is then passed through the gel. The pieces of DNA carry negative charges and move towards the positively charged electrode positioned at the other end of the gel. The smaller fragments move through the gel faster than the larger fragments and, consequently, travel further up the gel.

The next step involves separating the double-stranded fragments into single strands by immersing the slab of gel in an alkaline solution. (The purpose of this step will become clear shortly.)

After this, a technique known as **Southern blotting** (named after Edward Southern who developed the technique) is used to transfer the DNA fragments on to a nylon membrane. It involves putting a thin sheet of nylon over the gel and covering it with absorbent paper towels. The absorbent paper draws the DNA fragments up into the membrane by capillary action with their relative positions unchanged. The fragments are then fixed to the membrane by exposure to ultraviolet light.

Hybridisation

At this point, a radioactive **DNA probe** is used to bind on to and reveal the location of a certain type of minisatellite that is known to be polymorphic. The technique involves immersing the nylon membrane in a solution containing the radioactive DNA probe. (DNA probes used in forensic science usually consist of one strand of a length of DNA (often part of a chromosome) made up of repeated sequences of bases.) The radioactive probe will bind on to or hybridise with **single-stranded** DNA fragments but only if they make contact with a specific sequence of bases that is complementary to the probe (adenine with thymine, cytosine with guanine). Excess probes are quite simply washed away and the process repeated with a different radioactive probe.

The final step in DNA fingerprinting consists of making visible the minisatellite regions that have been picked up by the radioactive probes. This is done by putting an X-ray film over the nylon membrane. The places where radioactive probes have bound to DNA fragments will emit radiation which will fog the film. This creates a pattern of bands known as a 'DNA print', which is not unlike the bar codes found on retail goods.

For forensic work, the probes used are commonly of a type which will bind only at one specific site or **locus**; these are known as **single-locus** probes. Humans have two copies of most chromosomes – one contributed by the father, the other by the mother. Each individual should therefore have two of each of each type of minisatellite. If they are of the same length they will both appear as one band. If they are of different lengths they will appear as two bands. Forensic laboratories commonly use three or four single-locus probes on a single sample, giving a DNA print with up to six or eight bands.

Analysing the results

Visual inspection is first used to see whether two DNA prints match. If there is a visual match, an automated scanning system is used to calculate the length of the DNA fragments denoted by the bands. This involves measuring how far the fragment has travelled through the gel, compared with the distance travelled by marker bands of DNA of known length. The DNA profile is then expressed as a set of six to eight numbers.

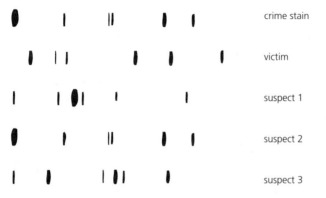

Figure 8.7 The DNA profiles show a visual match between the crime stain and suspect 2

The next step consists of calculating the odds of somebody else in the population having the same DNA profile as the suspect. This typically works out to be 1 in 30 for a single band. However, by multiplying together the odds from eight bands, analysts can generate odds of hundreds of millions to 1.

Problems with contamination

DNA fingerprints have been widely used to settle paternity disputes, to help identify rapists and murderers, and even to establish the ownership of a prized pedigree cat. Until 1989, DNA evidence was regarded as unassailable. Since then, however, scientists have questioned the reliability and accuracy of tests carried out in some forensic laboratories. The criticisms have largely been directed not against the underlying theory but against the standards of practice in some laboratories and their interpretation of data.

The problem is that forensic samples are rarely pure. A blood sample may be contaminated with fabric and dyes from clothing. Tissue samples are also inevitably contaminated with DNA from bacteria and fungi. Contaminants, it is argued, could react with the restriction enzymes causing them to cut the DNA at the wrong places. Ions mixed in with the contaminants could affect the charges on the DNA fragments, thus causing them to travel through the gel at a faster or slower speed. If the forensic scientist was slow in collecting the sample, the DNA could have decomposed so that some sites attacked by the restriction enzymes could have been lost. This could result in longer or shorter fragments being produced. Such criticisms have led to a greater understanding of the strengths and weaknesses of DNA profiling and more stringent quality control in forensic laboratories.

Questions

5 What is DNA fingerprinting or profiling?
6 What parts of the DNA molecule are particularly useful for forensic work? Explain your answer.
7 Explain the limitations of DNA profiling.

Cystic fibrosis

Cystic fibrosis is a common, fatal genetic disease that strikes mostly Caucasian people. It afflicts those who have inherited two defective copies (one contributed by each parent) of the **cystic fibrosis gene** or, to give the gene its full name, the **cystic fibrosis transmembrane conductance regulator (CFTR) gene**. One in 20 Caucasians are carriers of the faulty gene and show no symptoms. About 1 in 2500 new-born babies has cystic fibrosis.

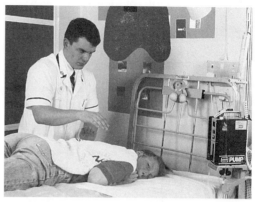

Figure 8.8 A gentle pounding of the chest (and back) along with antibiotics is the standard treatment for cystic fibrosis, but hope in the form of gene therapy is on the way

The protein coded by the normal CFTR gene pumps chloride ions out of the cells in the mucous membranes that line the lungs, intestines, pancreas and bile ducts. The water that flows out with the ions keeps the membrane lining smooth and wet. When the gene is defective, the chloride ions stay inside the epithelial cells and the mucous membrane is consequently dry. The effect is to cause an accumulation of a thick layer of sticky mucus in the lungs, making them very susceptible to infection by bacteria. The secretion of digestive juices by the pancreatic cells is also blocked by the accumulation of mucus in the pancreatic ducts. Identifiable symptoms of the disease include excessive salt in the sweat, difficulty with breathing and severe digestive disorders.

The disease routinely kills children in infancy but an increasing number of sufferers now live until their 30s. Advances in therapy have made the outlook brighter for sufferers but, for a biochemical cure, it would be necessary, in the first instance, to identify the defective gene responsible for the disease.

The search for the defective gene

The search for the cystic fibrosis gene began in earnest around 1980. Teams of researchers in various parts of the US, Canada and Europe began by collecting blood samples from patients with the disease and also from their unaffected relatives. By comparing the DNA of the unaffected relatives with those of the sufferers, the researchers were able to trace the cystic fibrosis gene to a section of chromosome 7.

(Humans have 23 pairs of chromosomes and, by convention, each pair, with the exception of the sex chromosomes, is assigned a number.) The researchers then began to look for physical 'markers', that is small pieces of readily identifiable DNA around that section of the chromosome 7 that were always inherited with the disease. These polymorphic markers vary from person to person – some are longer, others shorter. The researchers tracked the markers using restriction enzymes that cut DNA at particular sites. Several different markers were tested and eventually two were discovered that were always inherited with the cystic fibrosis gene. The gene they were looking for clearly lay between the two markers.

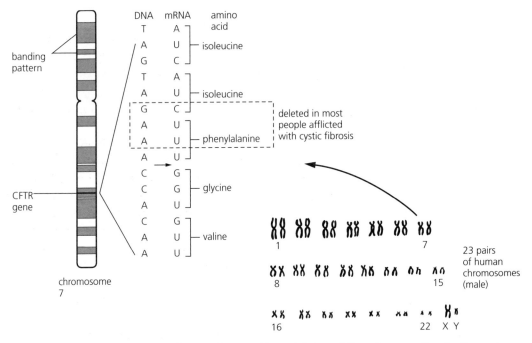

Figure 8.9 Cystic fibrosis is most frequently caused by a deletion of three bases coding for the amino acid phenylalanine in the CFTR gene on chromosome 7

In 1989, after nearly 10 years of research, the elusive gene was eventually isolated and **sequenced** (i.e., its base sequence was determined). The abnormality turned out to be a **mutation** consisting of **a deletion of three nucleotides** from the gene. The loss of those three nucleotides meant that the protein coded for by the mutant gene lacked the amino acid phenylalanine at position 508.

Genetic screening

DNA probes as diagnostic tools

Having sequenced a faulty gene, the next task is to develop a method of screening individuals who might be carriers of the faulty gene. The principal tools for genetic screening are **DNA probes**. A DNA probe consists of a short length of DNA that is used as a reagent to detect other DNA by means of a **hybridisation reaction**.

DNA is a double-helical molecule. The two strands of DNA are held together by weak interactions known as hydrogen bonds. The two strands can be separated if DNA is denatured by heat or chemical treatment. If the denatured DNA is then cooled, the two strands will spontaneously recombine to become a double-stranded molecule. Single-stranded DNA from **different sources** can bind or **hybridise** by hydrogen bonding to form double helices provided their bases are complementary, that is, adenine from one strand pairs with thymine on the other strand and cytosine with guanine; if the strands are not complementary, hybridisation does not occur.

An outline of the process

To detect target DNA (to continue our previous example – the mutant cystic fibrosis gene), a DNA probe is synthesised in the chemical laboratory to have a sequence of bases complementary with the target DNA's sequence. To clone the probe (and thus have lots of them for carrying out several tests), the segment of DNA is spliced into a plasmid, which is then introduced into bacteria. The multiplied probes are then extracted from the bacteria and 'labelled' by attaching an enzyme, a fluorescent dye or a radioactive atom.

The starting point for a genetic screening test is a sample of body fluids (e.g. sputum, urine or a drop of blood from a pin prick) as there are always a few nucleated cells in body fluids. A technique known as the **polymerase chain reaction (PCR)** is then used to amplify the extracted DNA into billions of copies of DNA, thus making it easier to detect the target DNA. The PCR technique will only make copies of existing DNA. The DNA is then cut up using restriction enzymes and separated according to size by electrophoresis. Using the Southern blot technique, the pieces of DNA are then transferred on to a nylon membrane. Heat or chemical methods are then used to separate the DNA into single strands. Labelled probes are mixed with the separated bands of DNA and if binding occurs, the individual either is afflicted with the disease or carries the faulty gene.

DNA probes have recently been used in a fast-acting and sensitive test for HIV infection.

Gene therapy

There are two main approaches to gene therapy – **germ-line gene therapy** and **somatic cell gene therapy**.

Germ-line gene therapy

This involves targeting the fertilised egg. It raises all kinds of ethical issues as well as practical considerations. Religious groups and anti-biotechnology activists are, on the one hand, adamant that tinkering with reproductive cells or early embryos to alter their genetic characteristics is positively immoral and should never be allowed. On the other hand, there are those parents, both of whom have two copies of a faulty gene responsible for a nasty genetic disease, who would like to have germ-line gene therapy so that their children and their children's children could be rid of the disease. Should they be denied, especially if, from work on animals in the years to come, the procedure proves to be simple and safe? Following a government advisory committee report in 1992, germ-line gene therapy has in fact been prohibited in Britain on the grounds that 'there is insufficient knowledge to evaluate the risks to future generations'.

Somatic cell gene therapy

Somatic cell gene therapy aims to deliver 'healthy' copies of the gene to the body cells that need it; for cystic fibrosis, it would be the cells lining the lungs. The idea is to insert normal genes into the cells in the hope that they would proceed to produce the protein needed for the chloride pumps to work properly and thus stop the lungs from producing the sticky mucus. Getting the 'healthy' genes into the cells, however, is a major obstacle.

The most widely studied technique exploits the ability of viruses to enter cells. The **adenovirus** is usually chosen as the gene carrier or vector because it has the natural ability to infect cells lining the human respiratory tract. To start with, genes that enable the virus to reproduce are cut off so that the virus is harmless. The normal CFTR gene is then spliced into the remaining portion of the viral DNA. The genetically engineered viruses are then delivered into the lung through the nostrils by means of an aerosol spray. The technique has so far not been very successful because the body's immune system soon learns that there are viruses lurking around in the body and proceeds to produce antibodies to wipe out the infection.

Another technique consists of packaging copies of the normal CFTR gene into microscopic fatty globules called **liposomes**. These are then sprayed to the lungs via the nostrils. The results have been quite promising. Patients receiving this type of treatment have shown encouraging signs of improvement.

Examination questions

1 An enzyme electrode can be used to measure the amount of a biochemical substance (analysate). The principle by which it works is that it contains an enzyme which converts the analysate into products which give rise to an electrical signal. The strength of the electrical signal may be measured with a suitable meter. The diagram shows a simple enzyme electrode.

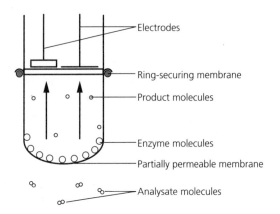

a By what process do the molecules of analysate reach the enzyme? (1)
b From your knowledge of enzymes:
  i) suggest how temperature might be expected to affect an enzyme electrode; (2)
  ii) suggest **two** advantages of using an enzyme electrode rather than a chemical test such as Benedict's test to determine the amount of glucose in a test sample. (2)

(total = 5)

AEB (Specimen Paper), 1994

2 The process known as genetic fingerprinting was first discovered by Professor Jeffreys at Leicester University in 1984. Since then genetic fingerprints have been widely used in criminal cases and also in establishing whether children are the true offspring of a particular man and woman. The method involves the use of a DNA sample, restriction enzymes, DNA probes and a technique similar to chromatography, called electrophoresis.
a Suggest why genetic fingerprints vary from one individual to another. (1)
b i) Define the term *restriction enzyme*. (1)
  ii) Why are restriction enzymes used in the process of obtaining a genetic fingerprint? (1)
c Suggest why *electrophoresis* is used in genetic fingerprinting. (1)
d What is meant by the term *DNA probe*? (2)
e State one other application of use of DNA probes. (1)

(total = 7)

O & C, June 1993

3 Read the following passage on the scientific, social and ethical issues surrounding cystic fibrosis and answer the questions which follow.

Cystic fibrosis: Gene therapy trials come to the UK

Cystic fibrosis (CF) is an ideal condition for gene therapy research as it is common, serious and affects the lungs, which are themselves relatively accessible. A number of scientific advances have come together to make gene therapy feasible for this disease: first isolation of the gene, second the development of systems for gene transfer into lung cells and third the development of the transgenic CF mouse (in which the human cystic fibrosis gene has been incorporated into the mouse genome).

What is CF?

Cystic fibrosis is the result of a defect in a single gene. In normal people this gene makes CFTR (CF transmembrane regulator), a protein which acts as a channel to allow chloride ions to move through the cells lining the lungs. This movement of ions carries water with it which keeps the airway wet and clean. In CF the abnormal CFTR does not work – and the chloride cannot get through the cell surface. As a result the airways are drier and less well protected against infection.

One of the most common single gene disorders, CF affects 1 in 2000 children born of European parents. The disease attacks the lungs, pancreas, gut and sweat glands. The problems in the gut affect nutrition but usually respond well to treatment. In contrast, the chest infections are more serious and difficult to treat.

The challenge for gene therapy, then, is to insert the normal version of the CF gene into the cells lining the lung so that they make normal CFTR which then allows normal chloride ion and water movement. The hope is this will prevent lung infection if given early enough, and might even slow down the damage in those who already have the CF lung disease.

Progress so far

Research into CF goes very fast. The gene was localised in 1985, identified and cloned in 1989, and shown to correct the chloride transport defect in 1990. A number of gene transport systems have since been designed. Those based on viral vectors have been pioneered in the USA and France while liposomes have been favoured in the UK. Liposomes are fatty globules which fuse with cell membranes and so insert any gene which is attached to them into the cell. Both of these systems have been tried out with laboratory animals and shown to transfer genes into the airway lining cells. Three laboratories have produced transgenic CF mice with airway ion transport abnormalities which can be used to test gene therapy. The mice were crucial for the British liposome trial: it was necessary to test liposome gene transfer systems in the mice to determine whether they were both safe and effective before moving to trials with people.

(Adapted from an article by Duncan Geddes in MRC News: Spring 1994, No 62.)

a What is meant by the term gene therapy? (1)

b What are viral vectors and how exactly might they be helpful in gene therapy? (3)

c Suggest why liposomes might be preferable to viral vectors. (2)

d Why is it important to have organisms such as the transgenic mouse available when developing new treatments for disease? (1)

e How could the CF gene have been identified and its exact location found? (2)

f As with the development of any new biotechnology, the development of gene therapy has ethical implications. What are the main concerns?

(2) (total = 11)

UODLE, June 1995

Suggestions for learning experiences

Activity 5.10 Designing and testing a urease biosensor (Investigation) *Advanced Biology Study Guide*, CG Clegg and DG Mackean with PH Openshaw and RC Reynolds. John Murray (Publishers) Ltd 1996, page 77.

Activity 29.5 Keeping in touch via the Internet (Demonstration) *Advanced Biology Study Guide*, CG Clegg and DG Mackean with PH Openshaw and RC Reynolds. John Murray (Publishers) Ltd 1996, page 354.

9

Microorganisms and disease

The term 'disease' literally means 'ill at ease'. It is used to describe any disturbed or unhealthy condition of the body which is unpleasant, often painful and sometimes fatal. Diseases may broadly be subdivided into two main types – **communicable diseases** (those that are caused by microorganisms and which can therefore be passed from one person to another) and **non-communicable diseases** (those caused by environmental or genetic factors). (See another *Advanced Biology Reader* in this series on *Health and Disease*).

Pathogens and disease

Disease-causing microorganisms are known as **pathogens**. For a pathogen to cause disease, it must colonise a region of the body, evade the host's defences and either by its growth or reproduction, or by the release of poisonous chemicals called **toxins**, directly injure the infected individual or elicit a host reaction that damages host tissues. An **infection** is said to occur when a pathogen successfully invades the host organism and establishes itself by multiplying within the body of the host. The host could be a bacterium, plant, animal or human being and the infecting agents could be viruses, bacteria, fungi, protoctists or animals such as parasitic worms.

Invasiveness

Some microbial diseases are highly infectious, others less so. The term **invasiveness** is used to refer to the ability of a pathogen to spread through the tissues of the host. This often depends on a number of conditions.

Attachment

The ability of a pathogen to attach itself to the tissues of the host is often a factor in determining whether it is successful in establishing an infection. For example, some virulent strains of *Escherichia coli* differ from non-virulent strains only because the virulent ones possess pili for attachment to the host's intestinal lining. Attachment prevents the pathogen from being swept away from a potential site of infection by the body's normal cleansing mechanisms. After attachment, some pathogens secrete proteolytic enzymes that break down the ground substance and basement membranes that bind epithelial cells together, thus allowing the invaders to dissolve their way through the body's first line of defence, the skin.

Slime capsule

The possession of a slime capsule or glycocalyx can also help a bacterial pathogen establish an infection. The slime capsule acts as a physical barrier preventing the host's defensive white blood cells from attacking the pathogen.

Adequate nutrients

Microorganisms, like all other living organisms, cannot multiply if a vital nutrient is missing or in short supply. For example, the amount of free iron in the human body is very low because various proteins in body fluids bind avidly to it. Bacteria that possess the ability to secrete molecules of low molecular weight (known as **siderophores**), which bind iron and have receptors on their outer membrane to capture the siderophore–iron complexes, stand a better chance of growing, multiplying and spreading through the body of the host than bacteria that lack this capability.

Destruction of host tissues

Along with the capacity to invade, the ability of the pathogen to produce harmful chemicals is another important factor in causing disease. These harmful chemicals may be subdivided into two types – **exotoxins** and **endotoxins**.

Exotoxins

Exotoxins are poisonous, soluble proteins released into the surroundings by many pathogenic bacteria. They are transported away from the site of infection by the host's bloodstream to produce their effects on other parts of the body. Being proteins, exotoxins can be inactivated by heat and by a number of chemicals (including iodine and formaldehyde). Some of the most poisonous substances known to humans (e.g. botulinum toxin) are exotoxins. Exotoxins are also highly immunogenic substances, which means that they stimulate the body's immune system to produce antibodies to neutralise their effects.

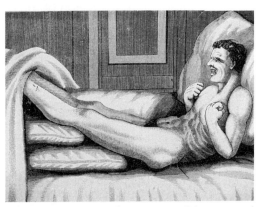

Figure 9.1 A victim of tetanus – a disease caused by an exotoxin which acts as a nerve poison. Notice the victim's jaws which are set in a characteristic grimacing smile, the clenched hands and the stiffening of the body due to the state of contraction of the body's muscles.

Exotoxins exert their effects in a variety of ways: some (like tetanus neurotoxin) act as nerve poisons whereas others (like diphtheria toxin) act by inhibiting protein synthesis. Some exotoxins are powerful proteolytic enzymes. One of the exotoxins of gas gangrene bacteria, for example, is an enzyme called lecithinase. It breaks down lecithin, an essential component of cell membranes. The so-called 'flesh-eating killer bug' *Streptococcus pyrogenes* secretes a variety of proteolytic enzymes, one of which damages human tissue by breaking down the common sulphur-containing amino acid cysteine. The staphylococcus enterotoxin (a food poison) acts by overstimulating the immune system into a frenzied attack on normal healthy tissues.

Endotoxins

Endotoxins are heat-stable, potentially lethal products liberated by the disintegration of Gram-negative bacteria. They are integral parts of the outer cell membrane of Gram-negative bacteria. They comprise a carbohydrate and a lipid that together form a large, complex molecule known as a **lipopolysaccharide**. The lipid part of the molecule, known as **lipid A**, is largely responsible for the biological effects of the molecule. The carbohydrate part, which protrudes like a microscopic hair from the outer cell membrane of Gram-negative bacteria, has a segment that is variable and specific to each strain of bacteria. This variable segment is also responsible for stimulating the host's defensive white blood cells into secreting antibodies against the endotoxin.

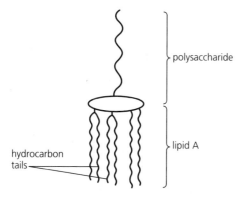

polysaccharide

lipid A

hydrocarbon tails

Figure 9.2 The structure of a lipopolysaccharide (endotoxin)

Endotoxins have both beneficial and harmful effects on the host. When Gram-negative bacteria invade host tissues and release moderate quantities of endotoxins, the effects are generally beneficial. The endotoxins stimulate production of chemicals called **cytokines** by defensive white blood cells that orchestrate a localised and controlled immune response that helps to eradicate the infection and enhance the body's resistance to new bacterial and viral infections. However, if the bacterial infection is severe and there are live Gram-negative bacteria multiplying in the bloodstream, white blood cells all over the body are stimulated into activity by mounting levels of endotoxins. The result is fever, increased permeability of blood vessels leading to a lethal drop in blood pressure and death due to circulatory failure.

The body's immunological response to infection

When body tissues are infected by invading microorganisms, the infected tissues defensively secrete cytokines, which cause blood vessels in the infected area to dilate. This explains why infected tissues look reddish and are said to be **inflamed**. The cytokines also stimulate endothelial cells lining the inner surface of the blood vessels to express proteins called **selectins**. These proteins, which function as homing antigens, adhere to the surface of passing white blood cells because there are complementary receptors there. Attachment stimulates the endothelial cells to spread apart slightly, thus allowing the white blood cells to squeeze out of the blood vessel and enter the injured tissue. These phagocytic white blood cells are capable of engulfing microbes and breaking them up with powerful digestive enzymes, a process known as **phagocytosis**. If some of the infectious agents are successful in evading the body's army of phagocytes, and the infection spreads, the race is then on for the microbes to multiply faster than the rate at which they are being destroyed by phagocytosis. If the microbes are winning and there are billions upon billions of microorganisms multiplying in the bloodstream, the unfortunate individual will feel very ill. This is especially likely if the bacteria are producing harmful toxins. If the individual subsequently recovers from illness, it is usually because the body's **immunological defence system** has been successful.

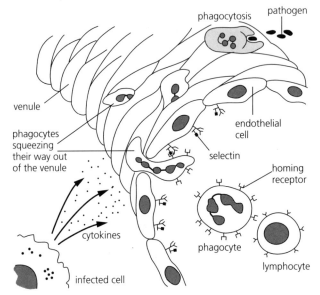

Figure 9.3 White blood cells being lured to a site of infection

The lymphocytes

The principal participants in the body's immunological response to infection are a class of white blood cells called lymphocytes. These cells prowl the body, moving between the blood and the lymphatic systems, searching for foreign or unfamiliar particles that might indicate the presence of viruses, bacteria or other harmful microorganisms or their products. If an intruder is detected, the lymphocytes mount a defence against it.

Lymphocytes can be divided into two main populations according to their origin and functional role in the immune system:

1 **T-lymphocytes** mature in the thymus gland and control what is known as **cell-mediated immunity**. The T-lymphocytes can be further subdivided into two classes – **cytotoxic (killer) T-cells** and **helper T-cells**
2 **B-lymphocytes** mature in the bone marrow and are responsible for **humoral immunity** through the secretion of **antibodies**.

Cell-mediated immunity

Whereas B-lymphocytes act against extracellular pathogens or their products, the T-lymphocytes are called into action against intracellular pathogens, that is those that are inside cells and are, so to speak, 'hidden away from view'. To do this, the T-lymphocytes must be able to recognise infected cells and avoid attacking healthy body cells.

'Self' and 'non-self'

When a body cell becomes infected by a microbe, the cell takes defensive action by breaking off a few peptides from the microbe's body and fitting them into grooves on special proteins called **human leucocyte antigens** (**HLAs**). The peptide–HLA complex is then brought to the surface of the infected cell where the foreign peptide, known as an **epitome** (meaning 'typical example'), is displayed to passing T-lymphocytes. Healthy body cells will display peptide fragments derived from their own or 'self' proteins.

All T-lymphocytes bear receptor molecules on their surface that are capable of recognising a particular foreign peptide. The receptors on any one T-lymphocyte are all the same. However, because of the great diversity of receptors made by the T-lymphocyte population, a match can always be found for any type of epitome displayed on the surface of body cells.

Cytotoxic T-cells

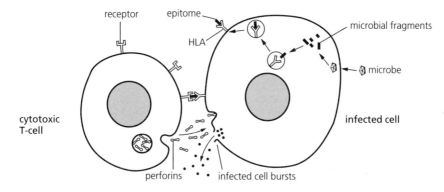

Figure 9.4 A diagram showing how a cytotoxic T-cell recognises and kills an infected cell

When a pre-killer T-lymphocyte recognises an infected cell bearing a foreign peptide on its surface, it divides repeatedly to form clones, daughter cells that mature to become **cytotoxic T-cells**. These T-cells are the most aggressive cells of the immune system. Their task is to screen other body cells for signs of infection. If a cytotoxic cell comes into direct contact with an infected body cell, it can kill the cell by 'punching' hundreds of cylindrical proteins called **perforin molecules**, which make holes in the cell membrane of the infected cell. The effect is to cause the leaky cell to lose control over the movement of substances through its membrane, thus allowing fluids from outside to rush in, leading to bursting of the cell. Cytotoxic cells can also release γ-**interferon**, a chemical substance that interferes with viral replication. They can also act by releasing molecules that serve as **signals**, effectively telling the infected cell to kill itself. The targeted cell responds by shrinking. It pulls itself away from its neighbours and then appears to boil as tiny balloon-like blisters appear and disappear at its surface. It then breaks up into fragments, which are quickly ingested by passing phagocytes.

Helper T-cells

Pre-helper T-cells are stimulated into dividing not by peptide fragments of intracellular pathogens but by fragments of bacterial toxins displayed on the surface of **macrophages**, a class of large, phagocytic white blood cells. The resulting daughter cell clones all develop into **helper T-cells**. These cells act by activating both the T- and the B-cell populations causing them to proliferate. They can, for example, by direct cell-to-cell contact, stimulate B-lymphocytes to divide and can, by releasing cytokines, stimulate antibody formation by the B-lymphocytes.

Different cytokines cause cells to do different things. γ-interferon, one of the cytokines released by the helper T-cells, stimulates macrophages to produce nitric oxide and toxic forms of oxygen which kill microorganisms engulfed by the macrophages. Another cytokine released by helper T-cells is **interleukin-2 (IL-2)**. This protein acts by stimulating activated T-cells to proliferate. Helper T-cells can also produce chemicals collectively called **opsonins**, which stick to the surface of pathogens, thus 'labelling' them for phagocytosis.

Humoral immunity

Unlike T-lymphocytes, which cannot 'see' entire antigens and can recognise only peptide fragments presented to them by HLAs, B-lymphocytes can recognise antigens like viruses, bacteria or bacterial toxins that are present in free suspension in the bloodstream. The B-lymphocytes are able to do this because their cell surface is bristling with membrane-bound antibodies that serve as receptor molecules, which can fit an antigen like a lock fits a key. Each B-lymphocyte bears only one type of antibody at its surface. However, because the body makes billions of B-lymphocytes, most of which bear antibodies that are different from other members of the B-lymphocyte population, the chances are good that some will bear receptors that will fit the antigens on the surface of invading microorganisms.

When a B-lymphocyte recognises an antigen and, additionally, receives activating signals from helper T-cells, it swells and divides rapidly to give rise to a huge clone of B cells. Most of these cells differentiate to become large, specialised antibody-secreting **plasma cells**, but some form clones of smaller, longer-living **memory cells**.

Plasma cells

The cytoplasm of plasma cells is richly endowed with ribosomes, thus enabling them to produce vast quantities of identical antibodies. Each plasma cell is capable of synthesising and releasing into the bloodstream 2000 antibody molecules per second.

Antibodies

Antibodies belong to a class of proteins called **immunoglobulins**. Each antibody molecule is made up of four polypeptide chains consisting of two identical 'heavy' chains and two identical 'light' chains. The four are joined by disulphide bonds to form a Y-shaped molecule.

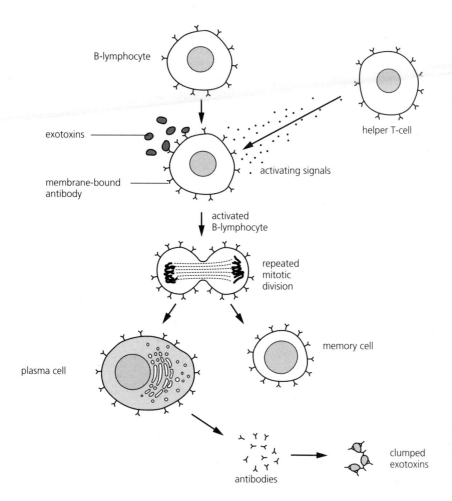

Figure 9.5 How B-lymphocytes defend the body against infection

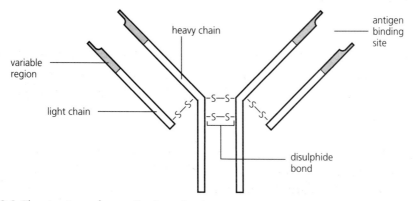

Figure 9.6 The structure of an antibody molecule

Antibodies bind directly on to antigens on the surface of microorganisms thus helping to 'label' them for destruction by phagocytosis; they are, in this way, acting like opsonins. They can also act by causing bacterial toxins to coagulate in lumps thus making them less harmful and more easily ingested by phagocytes.

Memory cells

All lymphocytes involved in the original or **primary immune response** to an infection die within a few days of eliminating the pathogen and are therefore no longer available should the body be invaded for a second time by the same pathogen. However, because of the existence of longer-living memory cells the body can respond much more quickly to a second attack. The memory cells can multiply rapidly and produce antibodies within three days of a second invasion. This is significantly quicker than the seven to ten days needed for antibody production against a totally new infection. Even so, the **secondary immune response** may not be fast enough to avoid symptoms of disease. It does, however, generate more memory cells so that in the event of a third attack, the response is even more rapid and there are usually no noticeable signs of disease. The person has, in other words, become immune to the disease. There are similar memory cells associated with the T-lymphocytes.

Some common microbial diseases

Staphylococcal food poisoning

Staphylococci are among the most important groups of bacteria that can cause disease in humans. Two species of staphylococci live on the skin and inside the nose of most humans. The white staphylococcus, *Staphylococcus albus*, seldom causes any trouble. However, living among the white variety are usually a few of the yellow variety known as *Staphylococcus aureus*.

If a few of the yellow staphylococci were to drop from the skin or nose on to cooked food left standing in a warm room, the staphylococci would feed, grow and multiply and within 24 hours increase their number to a few million. By then, the food may be 'a bit off' but still seem quite good to eat. If this badly contaminated, toxin-laden food is eaten, the unfortunate individual could be in for a bout of rather unpleasant food poisoning.

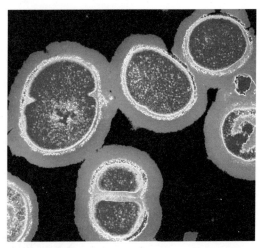

Figure 9.7 *Staphylococcus aureus* – a common cause of food poisoning

As it grows, *S. aureus* releases one or more exotoxins (named A, B, C, D and E). The exotoxins (or enterotoxins) are unusual in that they are relatively heat-resistant proteins and can withstand boiling for 30 minutes at 100 °C. Biologically, they act as **superantigens** by stimulating certain white blood cells called T lymphocytes to release IL-2. This substance stimulates proliferation of T-lymphocytes. The result is an overabundance of IL-2 in the blood. The brain responds to high levels of IL-2 by triggering a feeling of weakness, fever, nausea and vomiting or diarrhoea. This usually occurs a few hours after ingesting the heavily contaminated meal. The individual usually feels better within a day or two because intestinal enzymes have by then degraded the toxins.

How to avoid staphylococcal food poisoning

High standards of hygiene are of paramount importance.

- Hands should be washed with soap and water after using the toilet and before preparing food.
- Anyone suffering from diarrhoea should not prepare food for others.
- People with septic wounds on their hands or face should also be excluded from handling food.
- Fresh wounds on the hands should be covered with plaster and rubber gloves should be worn.
- Food should be eaten shortly after cooking while it is still hot or promptly cooled and kept covered at a low temperature until it is required.

Salmonella food poisoning

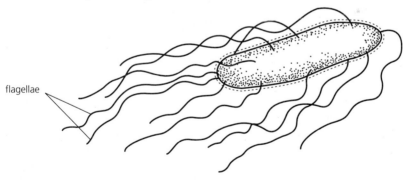

flagellae

Figure 9.8 A *Salmonella* bacterium – a common cause of food poisoning

Salmonella is a genus of flagellated, rod-shaped Gram-negative bacteria. There are many species all of which are potential pathogens. *Salmonella* is widely distributed among farm animals (chickens, ducks, turkeys, pigs and cattle). Infected animals (including humans) excrete *Salmonella* in their faeces. Since 1985, a virulent, very invasive strain called *S. enteriditis* has become the most frequently reported cause of *Salmonella* food poisoning. The pathogen finds its way into poultry most probably through contaminated soya feedstock. It multiplies within the gut, invades the bloodstream and may even colonise the oviduct of egg-laying hens. Both the egg yolk and the egg albumen of infected hens are as a result contaminated.

Live S. enteriditis have been recovered from eggs taken straight out of a refrigerator and then boiled for 8 minutes or fried 'sunny-side up'. In both these experiments, the yolk temperature did not reach 80 °C, the temperature needed to kill Salmonella. Food scientists warn that eggs should be kept in a refrigerator, then allowed to warm to room temperature before boiling for at least nine minutes. Alternatively, they should be fried both sides until the yolk has solidified.

Of far greater importance is the contamination of poultry meat by Salmonella. To quote the words of an eminent food scientist, 'Salmonella in eggs probably causes 300–400 food poisoning cases in Britain per year but Salmonella in contaminated poultry meat causes that many cases in a week'. The meat gets inevitably cross-contaminated with gut-dwelling Salmonella during preparation of the carcass.

Symptoms of Salmonella food poisoning usually appear quite suddenly within 12–24 hours of eating the contaminated food. There is a feeling of nausea followed by fever, diarrhoea or vomiting. The illness is usually mild, occasionally serious (especially in the young, infirm or elderly) but now, thanks to antibiotics, it is rarely fatal.

A few useful rules for avoiding bacterial cross-contamination around the kitchen

- Meat that is being thawed should never be placed on a rack above other foods because water containing live pathogens could drip down on to the food below.
- Deep-frozen meat should be left to completely thaw before cooking. If the meat is not completely thawed, cooking will merely continue the thawing process, leaving the internal temperature of the meat not high enough to kill live pathogens.
- Large joints should be cooked at a high enough temperature and for a sufficiently long period of time to ensure that any live pathogens present in the meat are killed.
- Surfaces and utensils used for preparing fresh meat should be kept separate and then decontaminated by washing with plenty of hot water and detergent.
- A old dishcloth used for mopping up after working with uncooked meats could spread infection around the kitchen if it is used to wipe other surfaces. A better alternative is to use a disposable paper towel.

Tuberculosis

Tuberculosis (TB) is primarily a disease of the lungs, although nearly any tissue or organ in the body (lymph, liver, bones, joints, central nervous system) may become infected and develop tuberculosis. The disease is caused by a small, rod-shaped bacterium called Mycobacterium tuberculosis. It is spread by airborne droplet infection when an individual with active tuberculosis coughs, speaks or sneezes. Airborne droplets of sputum, each containing hundreds of live tubercle bacilli, may be breathed into the lungs to cause infection in other individuals. The pathogen may also enter through the alimentary canal when infected milk is drunk. Most people infected with M. tuberculosis do not, however, become ill immediately. Only if the body's defensive immune system is weakened, for example by malnutrition or illness, will the infection develop into active tuberculosis.

To cause disease, the pathogen must first evade the body's defences. It must avoid being engulfed by phagocytic white blood cells that roam the tissues of the lungs in search of invading microorganisms. The bacilli must then multiply and establish a few granular sites of infection (known as **tubercles**) within the tissues of the lungs. Each tubercle consists of a centre of dead cells and tissues, cheese-like in appearance, that contains numerous tubercle bacilli. In susceptible individuals, the tubercular lesions may spread causing damage to large areas of the lungs.

Active tuberculosis is generally accompanied by a feeling of listlessness or fatigue, followed by fever, weight loss and a persistent cough. As the coughing gets worse, the individual's health deteriorates and there may be blood in the sputum due to erosion of adjacent blood vessels by the spreading of tubercle lesions in the lungs. An X-ray of the lungs will reveal typical shadows caused by clusters of tubercle nodules or lesions. The proportion of lung tissues available for gas exchange decreases and if the disease is untreated the patient dies through ventilatory failure. Treatment is with a combination of anti-TB drugs, including antibiotics.

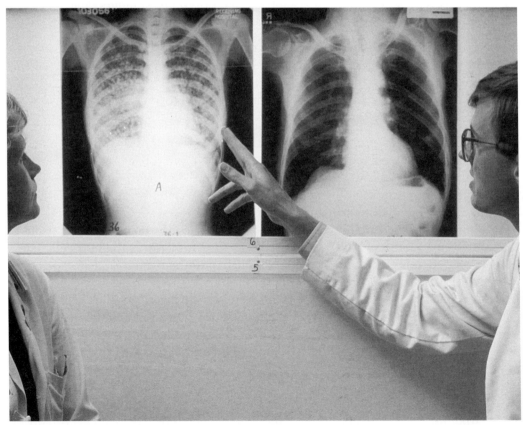

Figure 9.9 Examination of chest X-rays for signs of tuberculosis

Candidiasis

Candidiasis is an infectious disease caused by a yeast-like fungus called *Candida albicans*. The fungus is present in the mouth, vagina and intestinal tract of most normal individuals and ordinarily does not cause any ill effects. It only becomes pathogenic if the body's immune system is weakened by disease such as AIDS. It can also be a problem for individuals under prolonged medication with broad-spectrum antibiotics. These antibiotics kill off a wide range of microbial co-inhabitants, thus allowing the fungus, which is unaffected by the antibiotics, to grow luxuriantly.

Areas of the body predisposed to candidiasis are the moist surfaces of the mouth, gastrointestinal tract, vagina, armpits, between the buttocks and in the navel. Candidiasis of the mucous membranes of the mouth or vagina is known as **thrush**. The symptoms include painful white fluffy patches resembling milk curds, overlying a red inflamed base. Oral thrush occurs most often in bottle-fed babies (whose immune system is underdeveloped) and in AIDS patients. Vaginal thrush is common among pregnant women and people with diabetes. Treatment is with antifungal antibiotics such as nystatin.

HIV and AIDS

Human immunodeficiency virus (HIV), the cause of acquired immunodeficiency syndrome (AIDS), is passed from one human to another in four main ways:

- by sexual contact with an infected person
- by the shared use of a hypodermic needle with an infected person
- by injection of contaminated blood or blood products
- by an infected mother passing the virus on to her fetus or to a suckling baby.

HIV attacks the body's helper T-cells. These are white blood cells of the immune system that play an important role in defending the body against invading microorganisms. These T-cells, or lymphocytes, have protein receptors on their surfaces that bind specifically to the glycoproteins on the surface of HIV. The T-cells need their receptors for their own purposes but the virus latches on to them and uses them like 'door-handles' to gain entry into the cell.

Having entered the cell, the virus disintegrates. Its genetic material, which is in the form of two strands of RNA, is released into the cytoplasm of the host cell. The enzyme reverse transcriptase, which comes attached to the two viral RNA molecules, then transcribes the viral genetic information into DNA. Another enzyme, integrase, then splices the viral DNA into a host cell chromosome, thus making it part of the host cell's genome (total genetic make up). The original infective virus, which now exists as a segment of DNA known as a provirus, may then pass through a period of latency as it awaits chemical signals to prompt it into directing the host cell to produce virus particles.

Given the appropriate signal, the cell begins to make more viral RNA and viral proteins. These molecules spontaneously assemble into virus particles, which then escape from the cell to infect other T-lymphocytes. The infected T-cell eventually dies because the virus and other cells of the immune system destroy it.

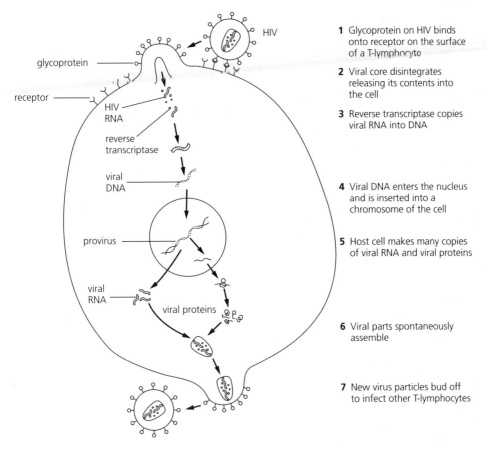

Figure 9.10 HIV's cell infection cycle

Labels on the diagram:

glycoprotein

receptor

HIV RNA

reverse transcriptase

viral DNA

provirus

viral RNA

viral proteins

HIV

1 Glycoprotein on HIV binds onto receptor on the surface of a T-lymphocyte

2 Viral core disintegrates releasing its contents into the cell

3 Reverse transcriptase copies viral RNA into DNA

4 Viral DNA enters the nucleus and is inserted into a chromosome of the cell

5 Host cell makes many copies of viral RNA and viral proteins

6 Viral parts spontaneously assemble

7 New virus particles bud off to infect other T-lymphocytes

Normal healthy individuals have about 1000 helper T-cells per cubic millimetre of blood. Loss of helper T-cells to below 200 per cubic millimetre of blood is a serious depletion. It is an indication that the body's immune system can no longer mount an effective defence against common infectious microorganisms. These normally benign co-inhabitors of the body can now proliferate wildly and the individual develops full-blown AIDS. Common AIDS-related diseases include:

- **thrush**
- **shingles** (painful skin blisters caused by the varicella–zoster virus, which attacks the sensory nerves of the affected areas)
- **oral hairy leukoplakia** (whitish patches on the tongue caused by the Epstein–Barr virus).

A number of anti-HIV drugs are available. Some act by blocking the viral enzyme reverse transcriptase; the widely prescribed drug zidovudine (AZT) works in this way. Others act by targeting other viral enzymes.

Questions

1 Explain why some microorganisms are more invasive than others.
2 What are endotoxins and how do they differ from exotoxins?
3 Give examples of human diseases caused by
   a a virus
   b a bacterium
   c a fungus
   and describe the effects of each of them on the individual. What steps can be taken to prevent these diseases?
4 What is meant by food poisoning? Name two microorganisms responsible for food poisoning and explain how they produce their effects. How may food poisoning be avoided?
5 Comment on the following statement: 'Tuberculosis can be a life-threatening disease but the microorganism responsible for the disease is not particularly invasive'.

Immunity

A person is said to be immune to an infectious disease if he or she can resist infection after exposure under natural conditions. The body's immunity is very specific. Immunity to the chickenpox virus, for example, does not confer immunity to the unrelated mumps virus. Immunity may be **active** or **passive** and acquired by **natural** or **artificial** means.

Natural active immunity

Immunity is said to be active when the individual makes its own antibodies. This is a common outcome of an infection and stems from the body's remarkable immunological memory. Its memory cells can not only recognise an intruder from a previous skirmish but also respond by dividing and producing antibody-secreting B-lymphocytes, as well as T-lymphocytes, to eliminate the intruder.

Naturally acquired active immunity may be life-long, as with some childhood diseases, such as chickenpox, mumps and measles, or it may be relatively short-lived, as in tetanus.

Artificial active immunity

Artificial active immunity can be acquired by giving an individual a dose of a weakened infectious agent (known as an **immunogen**). This process is known as **immunisation** (or **vaccination**). The weakened agent is introduced into the body by injection or taken orally. The body responds to its presence by producing antibodies that are capable of neutralising the virulent organism or agent of disease. The vaccine does not in itself cause disease because the agent has been weakened by mutation or killed or rendered harmless in some other way (see Vaccination and vaccines, opposite).

Passive immunity

Passive immunity involves the transfer of antibodies from one host to another. It offers only temporary protection because the antibodies slowly break down in the bloodstream. Natural passive immunity can be conferred by a mother to a child by the transfer of antibodies across the placenta or in her first secretions of breast milk (known as colostrum).

Sometimes, in an emergency, specific pre-formed antibodies extracted from the blood of humans, horses or cows may be given by injection to treat people exposed to poisons. For example, the bite of a king cobra can kill by paralysis within two hours of being bitten. The victim's life can be saved by giving an injection of **antivenin**, a serum containing antibodies against the neurotoxin present in cobra venom. Antivenin is obtained by 'milking' a king cobra and injecting a very small, non-lethal dose into a horse. The horse responds by producing antibodies against the cobra venom. The dose is later gradually increased to stimulate further production of antibodies. The serum (blood plasma without the blood clotting factors) extracted from the horse's blood is a rich source of antibodies. Passive immunisations are also used to temporarily protect travellers to countries where infectious hepatitis B is prevalent.

Vaccination and vaccines

There is a well-known saying that 'prevention is better than cure'. For a communicable disease, the simplest, safest and most cost-effective method of prevention is vaccination. Immunisations of one sort or another have been practised for hundreds of years.

The Chinese have, for centuries, been known to give a powder, made from the dried crusts shed by patients recovering from smallpox, to children to inhale. In the Middle East and in Africa, people who sought protection from the dreadful disease smallpox were given fresh material, taken from smallpox lesions of someone recovering from the disease, to rub on to a cut or scratch in their skin. This highly dangerous practice was intended to cause a mild case of the disease that would then hopefully result in immunity. Many did get immunised but some suffered the full effects of the terrible disease.

In 1796, an English doctor named Edward Jenner (1749–1823) made an astute observation. During Jenner's day, smallpox was very common, and many people died from it. Those that survived were severely disfigured with deeply marked holes called pock-marks on their skin. Jenner noticed that only the milkmaids had lovely smooth skins; this puzzled him. On making further enquiries, he discovered that most milkmaids had, at some stage in their lives, caught from cows a related disease called cowpox. Jenner reasoned that perhaps, having caught cowpox, the milkmaids had become immune to the more dangerous smallpox.

Jenner decided to carry out a very daring experiment (which for ethical reasons would have been totally unacceptable today). With a thorn, he made two scratches in the arm of a healthy boy. On to the wound, he smeared pus taken from a sore of a milkmaid who was having cowpox. The boy, as expected, developed cowpox. When the boy had recovered, Jenner took him to visit patients suffering from smallpox. Days passed and the boy did not show signs of disease. Was he now immune to smallpox? Jenner decided that there was only one way to find out. He once again made two scratches on the boy's arm but this time he smeared fresh material taken from a pustule of a patient with smallpox. Weeks passed and nothing happened. Jenner was now sure that he had found a way of preventing smallpox.

At first people were afraid and suspicious of his methods but fear of the real disease led many to allow Jenner to vaccinate them against smallpox. The term 'vaccination' is derived from the Latin word *vacca* meaning cow.

Figure 9.11 A statue of Edward Jenner (1749–1823) transferring fresh matter taken from a cowpox pustule on to scratches in the arm of a boy

Figure 9.12 An early nineteenth-century etching by James Gilray, illustrating the public's apprehension with cowpox vaccination

The aim in vaccinations is to use a harmless or weakened form of the infectious agent to stimulate production of antibodies that would protect the body against invasion by the virulent form of the pathogen. Vaccines are inoculable preparations containing antigens in a harmless form. Vaccines exploit the body's ability to 'remember' an antigen. The vaccines in use today can be subdivided into the following types:

- live attenuated organisms
- killed bacteria and viruses
- inactivated toxins
- subunit vaccines
- naked DNA.

Live attenuated organisms

The immune system sometimes requires a powerful stimulus before it will respond by producing antibodies. This is why a number of commonly used vaccines, including those targeted at measles, mumps and rubella, are based on live attenuated viruses. The term 'attenuated' means 'weakened'. Bacteria or viruses can be attenuated by growing them over a prolonged period of time in conditions that are different from those provided by their natural host. For example, if the influenza virus, which normally infects human cells, is cultured on chick embryos only a few embryos may at first become infected. However, if the egg fluid from the infected embryos (which contains live viruses) is used to infect a further batch of chick embryos and the process is repeated, the viruses will, over time, mutate and become better adapted to growing on chick cells. Such mutants may also, over time, become less and less adapted to killing human cells. It is these mutant microbes that are said to be attenuated and which are used in vaccines to provoke an immune response. Attenuations may also be achieved by prolonged seral culture under unusual conditions, such as high or low temperatures or oxygen-free surroundings. The use of whole, live microorganisms in vaccines is, however, not entirely without risk. Occasionally, an attenuated organism mutates back into a virulent form. This explains why the occasional child, after taking oral polio vaccine (which contains live attenuated viruses) gets polio.

Killed bacteria and viruses

Several widely used vaccines including those targeted at rabies and pertussis (whooping cough) are based on killed microorganisms. Viruses or bacteria are inactivated or 'killed' by treatment with chemicals such as formaldehyde or by radiation. The treatment does not affect the antigenic properties of their surface structures, which are, consequently, still capable of inducing an immune response.

Inactivated toxins

Some vaccines consist of chemically modified versions of bacterial toxins. These inactivated toxins are known as **toxoids**. Examples include vaccines against diphtheria and tetanus.

Subunit vaccines

Using molecular techniques now available to scientists, a new class of vaccines has recently become available. These are vaccines that use the antigenic subunits of the pathogens rather than the pathogens themselves. This eliminates the threat of an inadvertent infection by the occasional 'rogue' organism. Subunit vaccines against several common diseases including hepatitis B, meningitis and pneumonia are now obtainable.

Naked DNA

An unexpected recent discovery is that DNA coding for a foreign protein can by itself act as a vaccine if injected into muscle. Muscle cells, being much larger than other body cells, are probably capable of using the foreign DNA for protein synthesis.

The muscle cell's HLAs are then thought to pick up the foreign protein for display at the cell surface to passing T-cells. Recognition triggers an immune response. Naked DNA vaccines are available against a wide range of diseases including influenza, measles and malaria.

Vaccine production in plants

Scientists are in the process of developing genetically engineered plants that would one day produce vaccines against diseases like AIDS. It involves identifying the antigenic parts of the pathogen and then inserting the genes coding for the antigenic part into a harmless carrier such as a plant virus. The modified plant virus is then used to infect susceptible plants to cause the plant cells to produce large quantities of modified plant viruses. After purification, the modified plant viruses, bearing the antigenic protein on their surfaces, could then be given to children, perhaps in the form of a puree, similar to baby food, to prime the body against invasion by the real pathogen.

The technology has already led to the experimental production of hepatitis B antigens by potato plants, but since cooking destroys the antigens researchers have turned to the banana plant. They are hoping to develop bananas that can vaccinate against a range of diseases, including hepatitis B, yellow fever, diphtheria and polio.

Questions

6 Give an account of the ways by which the human body defends itself against invading microorganisms.
7 What do you understand by the term 'immunity'? Describe the different ways by which immunity can be achieved.
8 Explain how Edward Jenner's work has contributed to our present day control over infectious diseases.
9 Explain why in order to have lasting immunity against some diseases, two or more inoculations are sometimes necessary.
10 Give an account of the role of biotechnology in the production of modern vaccines.

Chemotherapy

The term 'chemotherapy' literally means 'treatment of the sick using chemical substances'. The science of chemotherapy, which deals with the specific use of chemical agents to treat parasitic diseases and cancer, has as its founding father the brilliant German physician named Paul Ehrlich (1854–1915). Ehrlich noticed that certain dyes were picked up more strongly by some types of cells and tissues and not by others. He reasoned that if he could find a chemical that is taken up selectively by a parasite, in quantities sufficient to kill the parasite but which is, at the same time, harmless or tolerated by the host, he would have found the 'magic bullets' needed to kill microbes living within the body of diseased individuals.

Ehrlich laid down three basic principles in chemotherapy. These are that the chemical should:

1 fix to the parasite before it can be expected to act
2 be harmful to the parasite but harmless or tolerated by the host
3 be capable of distribution to what ever part of the body the parasite may be hiding in and in a lethal enough concentration to kill it.

Figure 9.13 Paul Ehrlich (1854–1915) working in his laboratory

Despite years of trial and error involving hundreds of chemicals, Ehrlich never found the 'magic bullets' he was looking for. He did, however, find a cure for diphtheria and an arsenical drug that was effective against syphilis. His ideal drug was in fact discovered several years after his death and it took the form of the antibiotic penicillin.

Penicillin

Penicillin is a powerful antibacterial substance produced by the common mould fungus *Penicillium*. It acts by inhibiting enzymes involved in bacterial cell wall synthesis. (See also Chapter 3, page 42.)

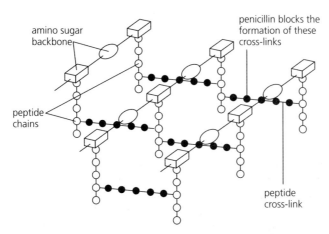

Figure 9.14 Diagram showing the structure of the peptidoglycan molecule and how penicillin weakens its structure

The bacterial cell wall is made up of layer upon layer of a giant complex polymer called peptidoglycan. This polymer has an amino sugar backbone consisting of two different alternating amino sugar units. A short peptide chain is attached to every other amino sugar unit. The structure is strengthened by cross-links that form between adjacent peptide chains. An enzyme, transpeptidase, catalyses the formation of the cross-links. Penicillin binds on to transpeptidase thus inhibiting the formation of the cross-links. The result is a bacterial cell wall that is soft and weak. The weakened cell literally bursts open because it is unable to withstand the osmotic pressures that develop as the cell takes up water from its surroundings by osmosis. Since human cells lack cell walls, they are unaffected by penicillin.

Other antibiotics

Inspired by the amazing success of penicillin as an antibacterial drug, searches were made for other similar substances in nature. Thousands of naturally occurring antibacterial substances were uncovered but many proved to be toxic to animals and were discarded. Others showed usefulness as potential medicines. One of the most notable successes was **streptomycin**, an antibiotic extracted from soil bacteria. It acts by binding on to the 30S ribosomal subunit causing a misreading of the mRNA codons during protein synthesis. **Erythromycin**, another antibiotic, acts by binding on to the larger of the two ribosomal subunits (50S), thus interfering with peptide-chain elongation during protein synthesis.

Antibiotic resistance

Although antibiotics have now been around for over half a century and have saved countless lives, bacterial diseases have not been eradicated and *Salmonella* food poisoning, meningococcal meningitis and leprosy are still around. One reason for their continued existence is the spread of antibiotic resistance. How did the resistance develop?

Spontaneous mutations

One possibility is that **spontaneous mutations** arose on bacterial chromosomes that fortuitously enabled the bacterial cell to acquire resistance. In the presence of the drug, susceptible cells died but the resistant ones were unaffected and lived. They proliferated and established themselves as resistant strains.

Mechanism of drug resistance

Resistance can involve the possession of an enzyme that cuts up the antibiotic. Bacteria that possess the enzyme penicillinase, which cuts an amide bond in the penicillin molecule, are resistant to penicillin. The resulting molecule, known as penicilloic acid, lacks antibiotic properties. Other mechanisms include chemical modification of the antibiotic binding site, synthesis of antibiotic-insensitive substitute enzymes and sequestering of the antibiotic so that it is no longer available for binding on to its target. Another mechanism involves molecules on the cell membrane that act as pumps for ejecting toxic chemicals and other unwanted substances including antibiotics. Although all organisms have these pumps, a recent study showed that drug-resistant *E. coli* had pumps that were remarkably effective in expelling different types of drugs.

How antibiotic resistance spreads

Drug-resistant bacteria are undoubtedly passed from one person to another within families and communities by direct physical contact or by the shared use of non-sterile utensils. In the vast majority of cases, when an individual falls ill and is prescribed a course of antibiotics the drug-resistant bacteria that survive the antibiotic treatment are 'mopped up' by the body's immune system and are thus eliminated. The problem arises when individuals with impaired immune systems are prescribed antibiotics. Because their immune system cannot eliminate all the drug-resistant survivors, these individuals could provide a breeding ground for drug-resistant bacteria. Such individuals may need additional drugs to assist their immune system to eliminate the drug-resistant microorganisms.

Incautious prescribing and improper use of antibiotics have also been blamed for the rise in antibiotic resistance. There is hard evidence, for example, that the widespread practice of feeding antibiotics to farm animals is adding to the problem. The evidence based on the comparative study of DNA sequences has shown that antibiotic-resistant bacteria living in the gut of pigs, sheep and cows have passed their antibiotic-resistant genes to distantly related bacteria living in the mouth and gut of humans.

How the gene for drug resistance is transmitted from one bacterial cell to another

Transmissible R plasmids

Plasmids occur in virtually all species of bacteria and most individual bacterial cells have them. Those that carry genes for antibiotic resistance are known as **R plasmids**. One mechanism that permits R plasmids and, therefore, drug resistance to be transmitted from one bacterial cell to another is bacterial conjugation. Such conjugations have been observed between 'male' and 'female' bacterial cells of the same species as well as between bacteria belonging to different species.

Transposons or 'jumping genes'

In 1974, another natural mechanism by which drug resistance could be spread at a disturbingly fast rate was discovered. Known as **transposition**, it involves short segments of DNA called **transposons** that have a natural tendency to 'jump' on to new sites on a chromosome or from plasmid to plasmid. Using this mechanism, which is quite independent of the normal method involving conjugation, genes for drug resistance can spread around to different plasmids and subsequently from one organism to another.

Antiseptics

Antiseptics are chemical substances which are applied to living tissues such as the skin or mucous membranes to prevent infection by killing or inhibiting the growth of pathogens. The antiseptic must be mild enough so as not to irritate host tissues. By contrast, disinfectants are substances that destroy microorganisms on inanimate surfaces such as surgical instruments, floors, walls and toilets. Their toxicity to humans is, therefore, not so significant.

Many chemical agents can be used as antiseptics. These include iodine, alcohol, bisphenols, potassium permanganate and hydrogen peroxide. There are a number of antiseptic products available on the market including creams, ointments, soaps and mouthwash.

Iodine

A dilute solution of iodine in water or ethanol (tincture of iodine) is widely used as a powerful antiseptic. Iodine is a broad-spectrum bactericidal agent that kills vegetative bacteria (but not bacterial spores) by combining with cellular proteins. It is used to prepare the intact skin for surgical operations but is too corrosive for use in the treatment of wounds.

Alcohol

Alcohol is an excellent skin antiseptic. It is applied to a chosen patch of the intact skin prior to using the area for giving a hypodermic injection or for withdrawing blood from a vein. Alcohol (ethanol or isopropanol) kills bacteria and fungi by denaturing enzymatic or structural proteins and/or solubilising membrane lipids.

Bisphenols

These are compounds, like hexachlorophene, that inhibit the growth of bacteria. They are used in a number of toilet preparations, including deodorants and antiseptic soaps. Surgeons use antiseptic soaps (containing 3% hexachlorophene) to scrub their hands before surgery.

Potassium permanganate and hydrogen peroxide

The antiseptic action of these chemicals depends on the fact that they are oxidising agents. Even slight oxidation of the cell proteins kills the cell.

Hypochlorites

Hypochlorites function as disinfectants by the formation of hypochlorous acid which in turn liberates reactive forms of oxygen. Many household disinfectants (e.g. Domestos and Milton) contain hypochlorites.

Detergents

Detergent molecules have a hydrophilic (water-loving) head and a hydrophobic (water-hating) tail. Their cleaning action depends on the fact that their hydrophobic tail sticks into grease whereas their hydrophilic head remains in water. Mild agitation separates the grease from the underlying material. Once lifted off, the greasy particles tend to become coated with detergent molecules. This coating prevents reattachment of the grease to the surface to be cleaned. Detergents can act as useful disinfectants because they are good cleansing agents and remove bacteria with the grease.

Evaluation of antiseptic effectiveness

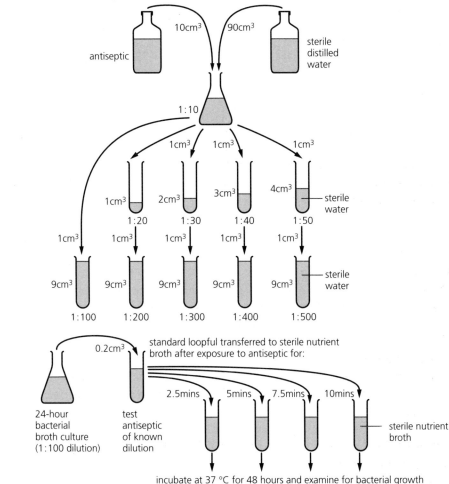

Figure 9.15 Evaluation of the effectiveness of an antiseptic

The effectiveness of an antiseptic (or disinfectant) as a killer of bacteria is assessed by comparison with phenol under defined conditions and against specific test microorganisms. A series of dilutions of the antiseptic under investigation is made using sterile distilled water. The dilutions are allowed to equilibrate at 17–18 °C. Each dilution is then inoculated with a fixed volume of a 24-hour broth culture of the test bacteria. (Usually 0.2 cm³ of a 1 : 100 dilution of the broth culture is used.) At intervals of 2.5, 5, 7.5 and 10 minutes, a standardised loopful of the inoculated antiseptic is then transferred to a separate fixed volume of sterile nutrient broth and incubated for 48 hours at 37 °C. A similar procedure is carried out for phenol. At the end of the 48-hour period, the tubes are examined for the presence of bacteria. The one particular dilution in which the bacteria are killed after 7.5 and 10 minutes' exposure but not after 2.5 and 5 minutes' will be the one used to calculate the antibacterial power of the antiseptic. There will be a similar result for phenol. These two critical dilutions, one for the antiseptic and the other for phenol, are expressed as a ratio known as the phenol coefficient:

$$\text{phenol coefficient} = \frac{\text{dilution factor of antiseptic}}{\text{dilution factor of phenol}}$$

For example, if the highest dilution of the antiseptic that kills the test bacteria after 7.5 and 10 minutes but not after 2.5 and 5 minutes is 1 : 200 and that for phenol is 1 : 90, the phenol coefficient would be 200 ÷ 90 = 2.22. The larger the phenol coefficient, the more potent the antiseptic.

Questions

11 What are antibiotics? Explain why penicillin is an ideal drug.
12 Explain the spread of antibiotic resistance.
13 What are antiseptics and explain their use in preventing the spread of infection.

Plant diseases

Like animals, plants are also subject to disease. A plant becomes diseased when its normal functions are disturbed and the plant is harmed by some causal agent, either a pathogen or an unfavourable environmental condition (e.g. lack of an essential nutrient). Several types of microorganisms can cause disease in plants. The two most important are fungi and viruses.

Fungi are responsible for approximately 75% of infectious plant diseases. Fungi are much more effective plant pathogens than bacteria because they are better equipped for penetrating the plant's protective epidermis. Their slender hyphae can force their way through wounds or stomatal openings to attack the living tissues of the host plant. Most fungi also produce reproductive structures called **sporangia**, which release numerous spores into the wind. The airborne spores can be carried long distances to infect other susceptible plants.

Damping-off disease in plants

Damping-off is a common soil-borne fungal disease of seedlings of the Cruciferae family. Several common vegetables including cabbage, broccoli, Brussels sprouts, cauliflower, kale, turnip and various kinds of mustard belong to the Cruciferae. The disease is caused by a fungus named *Pythium*. *Pythium* will attack newly germinated seedlings grown crowded together especially in damp conditions. The fungal hyphae penetrate the stems at ground level by secreting pectinases which break down the middle lamella that binds adjacent host cells together. During the early stages of the attack, the hyphae do not enter the host cells but permeate the intercellular spaces.

The diseased seedling wilts, collapses and dies from soft rot just above ground level, producing what is known as a 'wire-stem' effect (Figure 9.16). After the seedling has died, the fungus continues to feed saprobiontically on its dead tissues.

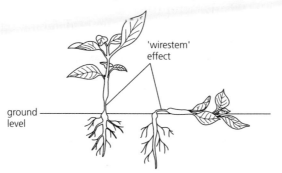

Figure 9.16 Seedlings with damping-off disease

Damping-off can be prevented by sterilising the soil before using it for sowing seeds. The seeds of susceptible plants should not be sown thickly and over-watering should be avoided. The fungus cannot easily be controlled because of its ability to feed saprobiontically and also because it attacks a number of hosts.

Control of plant diseases

The control of plant diseases can be broadly subdivided into different methods:

- cultural
- chemical
- genetic.

Cultural methods

Cultural control measures involve applications of the principles of **exclusion**, **eradication** and **protection**.

Exclusion

The aim in exclusion is to keep the pathogen away from the susceptible host plant. In practice this involves:

- disinfecting plants or seeds before planting
- using seeds or planting stock that are certified to be disease free
- sorting and discarding bulbs, corms or other parts that look suspect
- passing laws and establishing plant quarantines to prevent the introduction of potentially destructive pathogens into a disease-free area.

Eradication

This is the elimination of the pathogen after it has become established within an area. It involves:

- pruning off the diseased parts of the host plant
- burning or deep ploughing plant debris
- crop rotation with non-susceptible crops to starve out the pathogen.

Protection

This involves placing a protective barrier between the pathogen and the susceptible host. The barrier may take the form of a physical structure (such as a net to keep out flying insect vectors) or a climatic factor (such as low temperature) or a cultural practice (such as growing on raised beds). For example, damping-off disease can be avoided by sowing not too thickly or deeply and in raised beds to improve drainage. Virus diseases of potatoes can be avoided by cultivation at higher latitudes where the climate is unfavourable for insect vectors.

Chemical methods

The aim in chemical treatment is to place a chemical barrier between the disease-causing organism and the susceptible host plant. It involves in some cases using a suitable insecticide or fungicide in advance of the arrival of the insect vector or pathogen. For example, seeds, bulbs, corms and tubers are routinely treated with chemicals (such as fungicides, disinfectants and nematicides) to eradicate existing fungi, bacteria and nematodes and to protect against pathogens already in existence in the soil.

Genetic methods – host resistance and selective breeding

Undoubtedly, the best and safest method of disease control is provided by plant varieties that are resistant to common diseases. The resistance may take the form of a thicker, waxy cuticle, the release of a chemical exudate that inhibits growth of fungi or the production of a toxin that harms insect predators. Many wild species have survived because they possess genes that confer resistance to common diseases.

One of the aims of plant geneticists is to breed disease resistance into cultivated species. This may be achieved by crossing a wild relative with an economic variety. The hybrid that results may acquire the gene or genes for disease resistance but it may also lose some of the desirable features of the economic variety. In order to retain more of the desirable qualities of the economic variety, the hybrid is crossed with the economic variety a second and a third time so that by the third generation only one-eighth of the hybrid's genes are derived from the wild relative.

In recent years a quick and comparatively easy way of isolating a desired gene from a wild-type relative has been developed by geneticists at Cornell University in New York. The technique combines recent advances in molecular biology with traditional methods of plant breeding. It involves the use of a detailed genetic map of the crop plant (e.g. tomato). Such maps are now available for most of the important crop plants of the world. The Cornell team used the genetic map to provide a 'uniform flat background' against which they could judge the impact of the few wild-type genes acquired by the hybrid offspring of crosses of the sort described above.

Scattered throughout the genetic map are a number of easy-to-detect genetic markers. Whenever one of these markers turned up consistently with a desired trait, the team could be sure that the gene coding for that trait lay nearby. Hybrid offspring possessing the particular marker would be chosen for carrying out further crosses with the economic variety, whereas those lacking the marker would be ignored. In this way the team was able to 'spot' the desired gene and, in a relatively short time, produce a new variety possessing the desirable wild-type trait (e.g. disease resistance) without losing any of the desirable features of the economic variety.

Examination questions

1 The graph shows the responses to **two** identical doses of the same antigen.

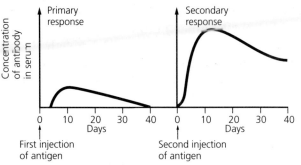

a i) Identify **two** differences between the responses shown. (1)
  ii) Briefly explain the mechanism which accounts for these differences. (3)
b How many days after the first injection should the second injection be given? Explain your answer. (1)

(total = 5)

AEB (Specimen Paper), 1994

2 The leaves of potato plants can be destroyed by a fungus disease. The rate of infection can be reduced by spraying with a copper-based fungicide.
  An experiment was carried out to determine the efficiency of the fungicide. Potatoes were planted in ten separate plots and at the first signs of infection, the plants in half the plots were sprayed with the fungicide and the other half were left unsprayed.
  The progress of the disease in all plots was recorded by sampling the plants and estimating the amount of diseased leaves using an arbitrary scale. Measurements were taken every 5 days. The results are given in the table below.

Day	Amount of infection/arbitrary units	
	Unsprayed plants	**Sprayed plants**
0	0	4.0
5	8.5	7.0
10	15.5	7.5
15	22.0	7.0
20	35.0	8.5
25	43.0	12.0
30	51.0	14.0

a i) Plot the data in a suitable graphical form. (5)
  ii) Using your graph, find the rate of infection of the unsprayed plants during the period from day 3 to day 12 of the experiment. Show your working. (3)
b i) Comment on the spread of infection in the unsprayed and sprayed plants. (2)
  ii) Suggest a reason for the results obtained for the sprayed plants. (1)
c Describe two disadvantages of the use of chemicals as fungicides. (4)

(total = 15)

ULEAC, June 1994

Suggestions for learning experiences

Activity 25.3 Bacterial growth in the presence of antibiotics (Investigation)
Advanced Biology Study Guide, CG Clegg and DG Mackean with PH Openshaw and RC Reynolds. John Murray (Publishers) Ltd 1996, page 288.
Activity 25.4 Disinfectants/antiseptics and bacterial growth (Investigation)
Advanced Biology Study Guide, CG Clegg and DG Mackean with PH Openshaw and RC Reynolds. John Murray (Publishers) Ltd 1996, page 288.

Index